GREATEST
WONDERS of the WORLD

Vikas khatri

Published by:

F-2/16, Ansari Road, Daryaganj, New Delhi-110002
011-23240026, 011-23240027 • *Fax:* 011-23240028
Email: info@vspublishers.com • *Website:* www.vspublishers.com

Regional Office : Hyderabad
5-1-707/1, Brij Bhawan (Beside Central Bank of India Lane)
Bank Street, Koti, Hyderabad - 500 095
040-24737290
E-mail: vspublishershyd@gmail.com

Branch Office : Mumbai
Flat No. Ground Floor, Sonmegh Building
No. 51, Karel Wadi, Thakurdwar, Mumbai - 400 002
022-22098268
E-mail: vspublishersmum@gmail.com

Follow us on:

For any assistance sms **VSPUB** to **56161**
All books available at **www.vspublishers.com**

© Copyright: *V&S PUBLISHERS*
ISBN 978-93-815883-0-7
Edition 2014

The Copyright of this book, as well as all matter contained herein (including illustrations) rests with the Publishers. No person shall copy the name of the book, its title design, matter and illustrations in any form and in any language, totally or partially or in any distorted form. Anybody doing so shall face legal action and will be responsible for damages.

Printed at : Param Offseters, Okhla, New Delhi

Prologue

Earth is a very beautiful planet. It has a store of treasures that can never be exhausted. The treasures of Earth are precious like gold and diamonds, but more precious than these are the treasures that fill a man with amazement, wonder, surprise and joy. The wonders of the Earth are many and of many kinds. Some of them are natural – nature formed them over time in a way that is beyond understanding.

Geothermal phenomena, like deep sea vents, volcanoes and waterfalls are of breathtaking beauty. Images of oneself haloed by rainbows formed high in the sky, take one's breath away. One can look and wonder at the marvels of the nature.

Some of the wonders are architectural marvels which, account for the brilliance of the human mind, its perceptive power and adroit endeavors. These were considered as some of the **greatest wonders of the world**, but not great enough to leave behind an indelible impression on human mind, they were lost to the other greater and stupendous works of the human imagination. The **momentous works** of art as and architecture by the humans and their ability to capture in realistic frame have baffled travellers and onlookers from times immemorial. With the advance of the science and technology, engineering skills and **construction facilities**, the human hands, out of there minds began to carve, edifices which made the world more pleasant and beautiful.

This book aims to present before the reader, 'a few' of the countless wonders our planet has to offer us.

Contents

The Seven Wonders of the Ancient World
1. Khufu's Great Pyramid 9
2. The Hanging Gardens of Babylon 12
3. The Statue of Zeus at Olympia 14
4. The Temple of Artemis/Diana 17
5. The Mausoleum at Halicarnassus 19
6. The Colossus of Rhodes 21
7. The Great Lighthouse at Alexandria 24

The Seven Wonders of the Medieval Mind
1. Stonehenge 27
2. The Colosseum 29
3. The Catacombs of Kom el Shoqafa 31
4. The Great Wall of China 34
5. The Porcelain Tower of Nanjing 36
6. The Hagia Sophia 38
7. The Leaning Tower of Pisa 40

The Seven Natural Wonders of the World
1. Mount Everest 43
2. The Great Barrier Reef 45
3. The Grand Canyon 47
4. Victoria Falls 49
5. The Harbour of Rio de Janeiro 51
6. Paricutin Volcano 53
7. The Northern Lights 55

The Seven Underwater Wonders of the World
1. Palau 59
2. The Belize Barrier Reef 61
3. The Galapagos Islands 64
4. The Northern Red Sea 66
5. Lake Baikal 68
6. The Great Barrier Reef 70
7. The Deep Sea Vents 72

The Seven Wonders of the Modern World
1. The Empire State Building 75
2. The Itaipu Dam 77
3. The CN Tower 79
4. The Panama Canal 81
5. The Channel Tunnel 83
6. The North Sea Protection Works (Netherlands) 85
7. The Golden Gate Bridge 86

Seven Forgotten Natural Wonders of the World
1. Angel Falls 89
2. The Bay of Fundy 91
3. Iguazu Falls 92
4. Krakatoa Island 94
5. Mount Fuji of Japan 96
6. Mount Kilimanjaro 97
7. Niagara Falls 98

The Seven Forgotten Modern Wonders of the World
1. The Clock Tower (Big Ben) 101
2. The Eiffel Tower 103
3. The Gateway Arch 105
4. The Aswan High Dam 107
5. The Hoover Dam 109
6. Mount Rushmore National Memorial 111
7. The Petronas Towers 113

Seven Forgotten Wonders of the Medieval Mind
1. Abu Simbel Temple 116
2. Angkor Wat 118
3. Taj Mahal of Agra 120
4. Mont Saint-Michel 122
5. The Moai Statues 124
6. The Parthenon of Athens 126
7. The Shwedagon Pagoda 128

The Seven Wonders of the Ancient World

The ancient Greeks loved to compile lists of the marvellous structures in their times. Though we think of the Seven Wonders of the Ancient World as a single list today, there were actually a number of lists compiled by different Greek writers. Antipater of Sidon, and Philon of Byzantium, drew up two of the most well-known lists. Many of the lists agreed on six of the seven items.

The final place on some lists was awarded to the Walls of the City of Babylon. On other lists, the Palace of Cyrus, king of Persia took the seventh position. Finally, towards the 6th century A.D., the final item became the Lighthouse at Alexandria. Since the it were Greeks who had made the lists, it is not unusual that many of the items on them were examples of Greek culture.

The writers might have listed the Great Wall of China if they had known about it, or Stonehenge if they'd seen it, but these places were beyond the limits of their world. It is a surprise to most people to learn that not all the Seven Wonders existed at the same time. Even if you lived in ancient times you still would have needed a time machine to see all the seven.

While the Great Pyramids of Egypt were were built centuries before the rest and are still around today (it is the only "wonder" still intact) most of the others only survived a few hundred years or less. The Colossus of Rhodes stood only a little more than half a century before an earthquake toppled it.

Khufu's Great Pyramid

More than any other ancient peoples, the Egyptians seemed to spend the best years of their lives, and certainly their best efforts, in preparation for death. The greatest toil, and the most perfect resting place, went to the pharaoh. It is a splendid tribute to all that industry that the Great Pyramid of the Pharaoh Khufu at Giza near Cairo is the only one of the Seven Wonders of the World that still stands.

Khufu's Great Pyramid

It would be difficult to imagine today's world without the Great Pyramid. It is more than 224 metres along each side, and 137 metres high - about the height of St Paul's Cathedral in London. It is a solid mass of masonry consisting of 2,300,000 blocks of stone, each about 2 ½ tonnes and, with the outer casing, weighing altogether nearly 7 million tonnes. All this monumental effort was expended by 100,000 workmen, using no draught-animals, no mechanical equipment and only the strength of their muscles to move each block. It took them twenty years to build Khufu's pyramid, in about 2,700 B.C.

Nearly are two more pyramids, and from an aircraft above them you can see south-wards a whole landscape of pyramids – each built to preserve one man's body under millions of tonnes of masonry.

The reason behind it all was that the Egyptians believed their pharaoh was a god – son of Re, the Sun-god. His spirit or soul (ka) could not survive in the afterworld unless his body was properly preserved, and for his journey to that world he would need his treasure, furniture, clothing, ornaments and all the regalia of his rank. All these things, therefore, had to be put into the pyramid with his body.

The pharaoh was not alone in needing the things of this world in his next life. The same was considered true of all Egyptians. A schoolboy dying prematurely would be buried with his exercise books; a carpenter with his tools; and for every dead person there would be plates of food in the tomb. So when, thousands of years later they re-emerged under the skilful probing of modern archaeologists, a way of life and a pattern of culture was revealed more vividly than any history book could portray.

We learn, for instance, that the pharaohs and their advisers knew that not even millions of stone blocks were sufficient deterrent to the tomb robbers of their times. Deep inside their tombs we can see how they dealt with the problem of thieves by building dummy corridors. Along these corridors they placed deep pits - traps from which there was no escape for any plunderer who fell in. How many ancient thieves died in this grisly way we shall never know, but the death pits are still there and your heart can still miss a beat as you look down to where one false step could lead you.

It is an awe-inspiring experience to walk, sometimes crouching, sometimes upright, through the sloping, dimly lit corridor inside Khufu's pyramid, where the pharaoh, the most powerful man in the world 5,000 years ago, intended that no human being should ever walk.

A steep passage leads to the pharaoh's last resting place, a soundless room furnished now with only a huge empty granite coffin. After the size of the pyramid, the room seems strangely small. The passage was sealed after Khufu's funeral by releasing granite blocks that slid into place to form part of the masonry.

What happened to the pharaoh's body? Curiously, from the very earliest descriptions of the Great Pyramid, the coffin room has always been described as empty. Perhaps, when the accumulated knowledge of twenty years' hard labour was being passed around by 100,000 workmen, tomb robbers were able to piece together a detailed account of the secret interior structure of the pyramid and work out a plan to rob it. Perhaps, too, they stole the royal mummy so as to leave no trace of their vandalism. Since Egyptians would consider that as soon as the mummy ceased to exist its soul would die, the irony is that the Great Pyramid was built for nothing.

Khufu's successor, it is believed, was his brother Cephren, who built the second great pyramid at Giza, next to Khufu's. Cephren's face is familiar, for it is the face of the Sphinx. Nearly 5,000 years ago this pharaoh had the Sphinx carved out in his own likeness, to remind Egyptians that their ruler was at one with the gods.

The third pyramid at Giza, the smallest of the three, was built by Menkaura. He is a pharaoh about whom very little is known, except that he reigned for a much shorter period than either of his predecessors Khufu and Cephren.

The Hanging Gardens of Babylon

Six hundred years before the birth of Christ, King Nabopalassar of Babylon was brought the news he had long been waiting for. His army, combined with the Medes, had at last destroyed Nineveh, capital of the brutal Assyrian Empire, and defeated the Assyrian army.

The Hanging Gardens of Babylon

Triumphantly, Nabopalassar prepared to build a great empire for his successors. How this was done is vividly reported in the Bible, which tells how the Chaldeans, as the Babylonians were then called, built their empire on the successes of war.

Nabopalassar died and his son Nebuchadnezzar, a successful soldier, succeeded him. Nebuchadnezzar's aim was to build Babylon as a monument to his glory. Fortresses and strongpoints were raised along its walls, a bridge was built to span the river and the fortified royal palace, reached by the Ishtar Gate, rose in splendour above the city.

Close to his palace Nebuchadnezzar built his amazing Hanging Gardens, which Greek visitors to Babylon described as one of the Seven Wonders of the World. The King made the gardens, it was said, to please his Queen, who was a Princess of the Medes — the same tribe that had allied itself to his father for the final overthrow of the Assyrians.

The Queen, so the story went, disliked the flatness of Babylon, and was homesick for the hills of her native land, so Nebuchadnezzar had his gardens laid out on terraces to form a man-made hill. The terraces were connected by steps 3 metres wide, and they were built in tiers held up by vast arches, raised upon other arches, one above the other to a height of 100 metres. A strengthening wall 7 metres thick surrounded the gardens.

Huge flat stones covered with lead were laid on top of the arches, in which the plants were grown. Elaborate building techniques prevented the earth's moisture from reaching the arches and undermining them, and all the gardens were watered by a pump, probably worked by slaves on the top tier, which drew water from the river below.

Everywhere there was water, cascading in waterfalls and trickling unseen into the lead-based flower beds to maintain the lush oasis. Thus the Hanging Gardens, with the pulse of summer in the air, glistened like a jewel in the bustling capital of Nebuchadnezzar's exotic empire.

As Assyria had fallen, so did the Babylon that Nebuchadnezzar built. It lasted less than a century before it surrendered to Cyrus of Persia. Today Babylon is a ruin, mouldering in the dry desert of Iraq, and all that remains of its fabulous Hanging Gardens, built to please a homesick Queen, are a few arches and an empty well.

The Statue of Zeus at Olympia

To the ancient Greeks, no greater god dwelt on sacred Mount Olympus than Zeus. He looked like a man and thought like one; he even had human failings that caused him tiresome domestic problems, but he was the supreme god. Zeus was indeed beloved by all the Greeks.

The Statue of Zeus at Olympia

Four hundred and fifty years before the birth of Christ, the Greeks decided to show tangible evidence of this devotion. They would build a temple at Olympia with a splendid image of Zeus. With a strong will they set to work. When the temple was finished, the Greeks asked each other who should create the statue of Zeus. Everyone agreed upon Pheidias, a sculptor of great renown. The fact that Pheidias was busily working in Athens was no bother - they would wait until he was ready.

It was a long wait. More than ten years passed before Pheidias could come wearily to Olympia. But when he saw the grand design that was intended for Zeus he must have been fired with wonderful ideas. In his little workshop Pheidias began to fashion a seated figure made entirely of gold and ivory. He fastened gold plates about a wooden core of timber to form the draperies, and used slices of ivory for the figure's flesh.

The god, adorned by all the arts of the ancient jeweler, engraver and painter, was seated on a throne. On his head was a wreath imitating sprays of olive. In his right hand he carried a winged statue of the goddess Victory, who was also made of ivory and gold and had a wreath on her head.

In his left hand Zeus carried a sceptre, with an eagle perched upon it. His sandals, like his clothes, were made of gold. His throne was covered with gold and jewels, ebony and ivory, and it had all sorts of beasts and images painted on it.

"Wonderful!" declared the Greeks, when they looked upon their enthroned Zeus, who was about eight times larger than a man. A celebrated orator called Dio Chrysostom, who went to see the golden statue, praised it even more. "The sight of the figure would make a man forget all his troubles, however worn out he might be with sleeplessness and sorrow," he declared.

Most of what we know about the Olympian Zeus comes from a few ancient coins on which it was depicted, and the writings of a traveller named Pausanias, who tells us: "It is said that the god himself bore witness to the art of Pheidias. When the statue had just been completed, Pheidias prayed to the god to give a sign if the work was to his liking, and straightaway a thunderbolt struck that part of the floor where, even to my time, stood the bronze pitcher."

Pausanias doesn't tell us, though, anything about the head of the god or the look in his eye, which must have been what a visitor would see first, coming through the doors at the end of the soundless temple and beholding the huge seated figure at the other end. A coin of the time shows that Zeus had long hair, falling straight down the neck, a full beard and a moustache with long ends falling over the beard.

The Romans called Zeus Jupiter, and it is said that their Emperor Caligula had a madman's plan to take the Zeus to the Capitol in Rome and to substitute his own head for that of the god. But, as the story goes, his workmen were driven away by terrifying peals of ghostly laughter that broke out when they laid hands on the throne.

What became of Zeus? Nothing is known. The figure must have perished at Olympia in an earthquake, or in one of the barbarian attacks upon fifth-century Greece.

The Temple of Artemis/Diana

Which was the greatest building created by our ancestors? One ancient writer is quite sure. "I have seen the walls and hanging gardens of old Babylon, the statue of Olympian Jove (Zeus), the Colossus of Rhodes, the great labour of the lofty Pyramids, and the ancient tomb of Mausolus," he writes "but when I beheld the temple at Ephesus towering to the clouds, all these other marvels were eclipsed." Another writer, declared that the temple "surpasses every structure raised by human hands."

Temple of Artemis/Diana

Five times the people of the city of Ephesus (in what is now modern Turkey) built a temple on the site where, at the fifth attempt, they created this spectacular wonder of the world.

They began the first attempt, it is thought, about 700 BC, the fifth, the masterpiece dedicated to Diana, goddess of hunting, was finished about 323 BC.

When the fourth temple was burned down there was real determination in Ephesus to build a spectacular replacement. The ladies of the city sold their jewels to provide funds, and kings in Asia Minor presented columns. Alexander the Great offered to pay for everything if the Ephesians would inscribe his name upon it as the dedicator. They refused, replying with great diplomacy that it was not correct for one god to make dedications to another.

The new wonder of the world became a hallowed shrine for many peoples. "All nations," said a writer, "deposit their riches in the Temple of Diana." Another said "The temple is a common treasury for all Asia."

One story told about this treasure house concerns a famous painting of Alexander the Great on a horse, which hung in the temple. The painter, named Apelles, was paid twenty gold talents for it, although Alexander didn't seem to think it did him great justice. But his horse, coming up to the painting, began to neigh at the horse in the picture as if it were alive. "You see, King," said Apelles, "your horse is a better judge of a picture than you are!"

In the third century AD the Goths, who became the scourge of the decaying Roman Empire, plundered and burnt the temple, and it then appears that people just lost interest in it. The worship of Diana had gone out of fashion, and by the fourth century the temple's ruins were being quarried for building material. Its scanty remains were finally drowned by a river that changed course, and thus the temple that eclipsed all other marvels' was finally buried under a layer of mud.

The Mausoleum at Halicarnassus

It seemed to Queen Artemisia that her heart would overflow with sorrow when her husband died. He was a handsome man in the prime of life and - if his portrait is to be believed - a man of quiet dignity. His loss greatly saddened the devoted Artemisia.

Mausoleum at Halicarnassus

The way she decided to perpetuate his memory and appease her sadness made people gasp with wonder. She built for him the most splendid tomb ever conceived.

King Mausolus, the husband of Artemisia, ruled a province of the great Persian empire called Caria. A modern Turkish port, Budrum, marks the site of the King's capital, Halicarnassus.

When, in 353 BC, Mausolus departed from the world to dwell with his gods forever, Artemisia sent to Greece for the best artists and designers. There was Scopas, greatest sculptor of the century, renowned for his gift of expressing passionate emotion and vitality in stone; Satyros and Pythios the architects; and Timeotheos,

Bryaxis and Leochares, a trio of sculptors second only to Scopas.

These and other great talents set to work at Artemisia's bequest. But, before they had nearly finished, the Queen died. The artists decided they would complete the tomb for their own fame and as a record of their skill. When they had finished, the tomb was considered one of the Seven Wonders of the World. It was called, after King Mausolus, the Mausoleum.

It was, we know, a rectangle, with bands of sculpture around all four sides. There was a colonnade of 36 marble columns supporting a pyramid of 24 steps and on top of the pyramid was a horse-drawn chariot. Probably the draped statues of Mausolus and his wife stood in the chariot - the crowning glory of the Mausoleum. All this soared to a height of 43 metres, and somehow the Greek artists had contrived to make it seem that the massive pyramid, held up by the slender colonnade, was virtually floating in mid-air.

Sadly, this didn't seem to impress the Knights of St John, who early in the fifteenth century moved into Halicarnassus, and were probably responsible for stripping the Mausoleum in order to build their castle. Only a few fragments of the Mausoleum were preserved. Ironically though, the grief-stricken Queen Artemisia, who wished to preserve her husband's name for all time, succeeded in a way she could never have imagined, for the word 'mausoleum' is now used for any ornate tomb.

The Colossus of Rhodes

"Few men can clasp the thumb in their arms, and the fingers are larger than most statues. Where the limbs are broken asunder, vast caverns are seen yawning in the interior….."

The Colossus of Rhodes

This is how in the first century AD, the Roman historian Pliny described the Colossus of Rhodes as it lay broken, tumbled by an earthquake, on the ground. What he was looking at was an immense statue of Helias, or Apollo, the sun-god of the Greek island of Rhodes.

The Colossus, made of bronze, was created by a sculptor called Chares of Lindus. The work took twelve years, from 292 to 280 BC, and a story is told that when Chares had nearly finished his task, he discovered an error in his calculations and committed suicide. If this is true, Chares must have set himself impossibly high standards, for the Greeks, who were renowned for their knowledge of human sculpture, declared the Colossus to be the most perfect model of a human form ever fashioned by man.

Chares received his commission to create the Colossus as a result of a war. In 312 BC Ptolemy, king of Egypt, was fighting Antigonus, ruler of Macedon. The people of Rhodes decided to join forces with Ptolemy, and their ships of war and trade made a significant contribution to the defeat of Antigonus. Five years later the Macedonians, still nursing revenge, sent a huge force of men and ships to lay siege to Rhodes. There were more men in this Macedonian army than there were people in Rhodes, so the odds against the Rhodians seemed fearful.

Nevertheless, for twelve months Rhodes repulsed attack after attack. At the end of that time, her cause looked lost. Then Ptolemy of Egypt, not forgetting how well the Rhodians had helped him once before, sailed to their aid and forced the Macedonians to withdraw.

Overjoyed, the Rhodians summoned Chares the sculptor, who had himself fought valiantly in defence of Rhodes, to commemorate their deliverance by building the Colossus in honour of their protecting deity, the sun-god Helias. As an extra memorial to the great siege, the statue was made wholly of metal taken from the engines of war left behind by the Macedonians.

The Colossus, however, was to prove a short-lived wonder. Fifty-six years after it was erected an earthquake shook Rhodes and the bronze giant crashed on to the harbour rocks.

Still more degradation awaited it when, in AD 672, the Arabs took Rhodes. With not much more than a glance at the statue, they sold it, one of the Seven Wonders of the World, as scrap metal to a Jewish merchant. It took the merchant nine hundred camel loads - 300 tonnes of bronze - to carry it away.

7

The Great Lighthouse at Alexandria

Ships of the ancient world sailing the Mediterranean bound for Alexandria always knew where to find the port. For the Pharos - the amazing lighthouse of Alexandria - was visible from 43 kilometres out at sea.

Pharos Lighthouse Alexandria

At the summit of the Pharos was a huge mirror. Legend says that in it one could see all that was passing in the distant city of Constantinople. The glass, it is said, could be turned to concentrate the rays of the sun like a burning glass and so burn ships while they were still 160 kilometres out at sea.

Fanciful though this may be, there is no doubt that the Pharos was an awe-inspiring work of wonder. It was built, about two centuries before Christ, in white marble in the form of eight (some historians say four) towers, one above the other and each smaller than the one below it. The light was provided by a great brazier kept constantly burning.

It was not the first lighthouse of the ancient world, but undoubtedly it was the father of them all. Pharos in various forms has been adopted as the word for lighthouse in many languages. In Latin a lighthouse is pharus; in Spanish and Italian it is faros; in French phare; and pharos has not been obsolete for very long in the English language.

When the Arabs conquered Egypt the Pharos lit the way for Moslem ships, which caused the Christian Emperor of Constantinople to send a spy to Alexandria to destroy it. The trick used by this spy was incredible. Approaching the Caliph, Al-Walid, the spy declared: "Sir, it is said that there is a wonderful treasure buried under the Pharos. It was put there by the ancients when they began building. No finer collection of gold and jewels than is in those foundations has ever been seen by mortal man".

The Caliph fell for the trick. Stone by stone the Pharos was dismantled. It was not until it was nearly half down that he suspected a plot. But, although they tried hard, the Arabs couldn't put back the work they had destroyed. And the final tragedy occurred when the famous mirror fell and was broken into a thousand pieces.

In 1375 an earthquake shook Alexandria and hurled the ruins of the ancient tower, a mass of formless stone, into the sea. There, on the seabed of Alexandria harbour, some of it still remains - all that is left of the great light that once lit the ancient world.

The Seven Wonders of the Medieval Mind

The medieval mind, just like the classical mind before it, was captivated by the wondrous things people had made. For much of the thousand-year period known as the Middle Ages, most Europeans lived in small, isolated communities; travel was difficult and often dangerous; and knowledge was confined to, and often controlled by men of the church. The great civilizations of Greece and Rome were long gone, but even so, some of their glory was still remembered. Travellers brought back tales of an incredible civilization in the East which sparked the European imagination.

Following the third century B.C. when lists of wonders were compiled, many scholars and philosophers modified these lists to reflect their own opinions. At some point around the Middle Ages, another list appeared - the medieval world's seven wonders.

The surviving list holds a particular fascination because only some of its marvels actually date from the Middle Ages. The list represents almost 4,500 years of human endeavor.

Stonehenge

Stonehenge is a prehistoric monument located in the English county of Wiltshire, about 3.2 kilometres (2.0 mi) west of Amesbury and 13 kilometres (8.1 mi) north of Salisbury. One of the most famous prehistoric sites in the world, Stonehenge is composed of earthworks surrounding a circular setting of large standing stones. Archaeologists believe that the standing stones were erected around 2200 BC and the surrounding circular earth bank and ditch, which constitute the earliest phase of the monument, have been dated to about 3100 BC.

Stonehenge

The site and its surroundings were added to the UNESCO's list of World Heritage Sites in 1986 in a co-listing with Avebury henge monument, and it is also a legally protected Scheduled Ancient Monument. Stonehenge itself is owned by the Crown and managed by English Heritage while the surrounding land is owned by the National Trust.

The Stonehenge complex was built in several construction phases spanning at least 3000 years, although there is evidence for activity both before and afterwards on the site, perhaps extending its time frame to 6500 years.

New archaeological evidence found by the Stonehenge Riverside Project indicates that Stonehenge served as a burial ground from its earliest beginnings. The dating of cremated remains found that burials took place as early as 3000 B.C, when the first ditches were being built around the monument. Burials continued at Stonehenge for at least another 500 years when the giant stones which mark the landmark were put up.

The Stonehenge complex was built in several construction phases spanning at least 3000 years, although there is evidence for activity both before and afterwards on the site, perhaps extending its time frame to 6500 years.

Dating and understanding the various phases of activity at Stonehenge is not a simple task; it is complicated by poorly kept early excavation records, except for few accurate scientific dates and the disturbance of the natural chalk by periglacial effects and animal burrowing.

The Colosseum

The Colosseum or Coliseum, originally the Flavian Amphitheatre, is an elliptical amphitheatre in the centre of the city of Rome, Italy, the largest ever built in the Roman Empire. It is one of the greatest works of Roman architecture and Roman engineering.

Roman Colosseum

Occupying a site just east of the Roman Forum, its construction started between 70 and 72 AD under the emperor Vespasian and was completed in 80 AD under Titus, with further modifications being made during Domitian's reign (81-96).

Originally capable of seating around 50,000 spectators, the Colosseum was used for gladiatorial contests and public spectacles. It remained in use for nearly 500 years with the last recorded games being held there as late as the 6th century.

As well as the traditional gladiatorial games, many other public spectacles were held there, such as mock sea battles, animal hunts, executions, re-enactments of famous battles, and dramas based on Classical mythology. The building eventually ceased to be used for entertainment in the early medieval era. It was later reused for such varied purposes as housing, workshops, and quarters for a religious order, a fortress, a quarry and a Christian shrine.

Unlike earlier amphitheatres that were built into hillsides, the Colosseum is an entirely free-standing structure. It is elliptical in plan and is 189 metres (615 ft / 640 Roman feet) long, and 156 metres (510 ft / 528 Roman feet) wide, with a base area of 6 acres. The height of the outer wall is 48 metres (157 ft / 165 Roman feet). The perimetre originally measured 545 metres (1,788 ft / 1,835 Roman feet). The central arena is an oval (287 ft) long and (180 ft) wide, surrounded by a wall (15 ft) high, above which rose tiers of seating.

The outer wall is estimated to have required over 100,000 cubic metres (131,000 cu yd) of travertine stone which were set without mortar held together by 300 tons of iron clamps. However, it has suffered extensive damage over the centuries, with large segments having collapsed following earthquakes. The north side of the perimetre wall is still standing; the distinctive triangular brick wedges at each end are modern additions, having been constructed in the early 19th century to shore up the wall. The remainder of the present-day exterior of the Colosseum is in fact the original interior wall.

3

The Catacombs of Kom el Shoqafa

Alexandria, Egypt, represented a melding of cultures in the late first century A.D. Traditions of Greece and Rome overlay the city, the cult of Christianity was gaining ground, and memories of ancient Egypt's great kingdoms still lingered. It was a place where people seemed to have a talent for combining rather than destroying cultures.

Kom el Shoqafa

Little of that "Paris of Antiquity" has survived above the ground. Below it, however, are haunting reminders of a culture that existed 1,900 years ago: the Catacombs of Kom el Shoqafa, "Mound of Shards." Carved out of solid rock, three levels burrow into the ground near the sites of the ancient stadium, and the long- vanished temple to Serapis, a Greek and Egyptian god. Many such catacombs once filigreed Alexandria's underground, but earthquakes and construction projects destroyed or obscured them. Only in 1900 was Kom el Shoqafa rediscovered after centuries - by a donkey that fell through a hole in the ground and into its access well. The animal, it soon became clear, had made an extraordinary archeological find.

An ancient circular staircase leads down into the catacombs. In the late second century, when Kom el Shaqafa was an active burial site, bodies were lowered by rope down the well formed by the spiraling stairs. The staircase ends at a landing vestibule, where two benches are carved into wall niches overarched by the cockleshell motif often found in classical designs.

A rotunda pierced by a six-pillared central shaft opens off the vestibule. To the left lies the *triclinium*, the funeral banquet hall where friends and family gathered on stone couches covered with cushions. Here they reclined while ceremonially feasting in memory of the deceased. Scholars believe that the catacombs at first may have served one family, but they were expanded into a mass burial site, probably administered by a corporation with dues-paying members. This theory could explain why so many chambers were hewn from the rock.

A staircase from the rotunda descends to the second level, an area eerily alive with sculpture. In the vestibule, two pillars are topped by the papyrus, lotus, and acanthus leaves of ancient Egypt, their frieze adorned by two falcons flanking a winged sun. Carved into wall niches are figures of a man, and a woman, perhaps the tomb's original occupants. The man's body assumes the stiff hieratic pose found in ancient Egyptian sculpture, but his head is in the lifelike manner of the classic Hellenes; the woman's stance is also rigid, but she sports a Roman hairstyle.

Three gigantic sarcophagi with lids that do not lift, rest along the sides of the chamber. Scholars assume that bodies would have been inserted into them from behind, using a passageway that runs around the outside of the funeral chamber. Further circling this central tomb chamber is a hallway with 91 wall niches, each one providing burial space for three mummies.

Returning to the first level, visitors can reach a separate set of tombs through a breach in the rotunda wall, unintended by the original builders. It leads to what has been called the Hall of Caracalla, where bones of horses and humans were found. The hall's name comes from an episode in A.D. 215, when Emperor Caracalla ordered Alexandrian youths to review, then massacred them.

The Great Wall of China

The Great Wall of China is a series of stone and earthen fortifications in China, built, rebuilt, and maintained between the 6th century BC and the 16th century to protect the northern borders of the Chinese Empire from Xiongnu attacks during the rule of successive dynasties. Several walls, referred to as the Great Wall of China, were built since the 5th century BC. The most famous is the wall built between 220-200 BC by the first Emperor of China, Qin Shi Huang; little of it remains; it was much farther north than the current wall, which was built during the Ming Dynasty.

The Great Wall of China

The Great Wall stretches over approximately 6,400 km (4,000 miles) from Shanhaiguan in the east to Lop Nur in the west, along an arc that roughly delineates the southern edge of Inner Mongolia, but stretches to over 6,700 km (4,160 miles) in total. At its peak, the Ming Wall was guarded by more than one million men. It has been estimated that somewhere in the range of 2 to 3 million Chinese died as part of the centuries-long project of building the wall.

Transporting the large quantity of materials required for construction was difficult, so builders always tried to use local resources. Stones from the mountains were used over mountain ranges, while rammed earth was used for construction in the plains. There are no surviving historical records indicating the exact length and course of the Qin Dynasty walls. Most of the ancient walls have eroded away over the centuries, and very few sections remain today.

Before the use of bricks, the Great Wall was mainly built from Earth or Taipa, stones, and wood. During the Ming Dynasty, however, bricks were heavily used in many areas of the wall, as were materials such as tiles, lime, and stone. The size and weight of the bricks made them easier to work with than earth and stone, so construction quickened. Additionally, bricks could bear more weight and endure better than rammed earth. Stone can hold under its own weight better than brick, but is more difficult to use. Consequently, stones cut in rectangular shapes were used for the foundation, inner and outer brims, and gateways of the wall. Battlements line the uppermost portion of the vast majority of the wall, with defensive gaps a little over 30 cm (one foot) tall, and about 23 cm (9 inches) wide.

The Porcelain Tower of Nanjing

The Porcelain Tower (or Porcelain Pagoda) of Nanjing, also known as Bao'ensi (meaning "Temple of Gratitude"), is a historical archaeological site located on the south bank of the Yangtze in Nanjing, China. It was constructed in the 15th century as a Buddhist pagoda, but was mostly destroyed in the 19th century during the course of the Taiping rebellion. However, the tower is now under reconstruction once again.

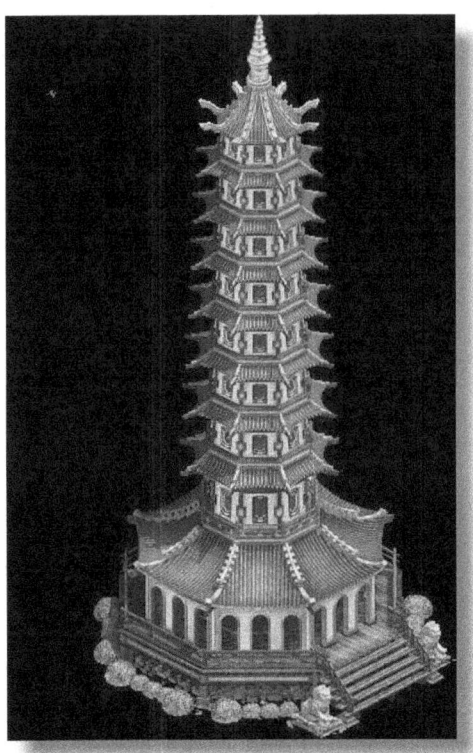

The Porcelain Tower of Nanjing

The tower was octagonal with a base of about 97 ft in diametre. When it was built, the tower was one of the largest buildings in China, rising up to a height of 260 feet with nine stories and a staircase in the middle of the pagoda, which spiraled upwards for 130 steps. The top of the roof was marked by a golden sphere. There were originally plans to add more stories, according to an American missionary who in 1852 visited Nanjing.

The tower was built with white porcelain bricks that were said to reflect the sun's rays during the day, and at night as many as 140 lamps were hung from the building to illuminate the tower. Glazes and stoneware were worked into the porcelain and created a mixture of green, yellow, brown and white designs on the sides of the tower, including animals, flowers and landscapes. The tower was also decorated with numerous Buddhist images.

The Porcelain Tower of Nanjing was designed by the Chinese Emperor Yongle shortly before its construction, in the early 15th century. It was first discovered by the Western world when European travelers visited it, sometimes listing it as one of the Seven Wonders of the World.

In 1801 a bolt of lightning struck and knocked off the top three stories of the tower, but it was soon restored. In the 1850s the area surrounding the tower erupted in civil war as the Taiping Rebellion reached Nanjing and the Taiping Rebels took over the city. They smashed the Buddhist images and destroyed the inner staircase to deny the Qing enemy an observation platform. American sailors reached the city in May 1854 and visited the hollowed tower. In 1856 the Taiping destroyed the tower in order to prevent a hostile faction from using it to observe and shell the city. After this point, the tower's remnants were forgotten and it lay dormant until a recent surge to try and rebuild the landmark.

The Hagia Sophia

Hagia Sophia is a former patriarchal basilica, later a mosque, now a museum, in Istanbul, Turkey. Famous in particular for its massive dome, it is considered the epitome of Byzantine, architecture. It was the largest cathedral ever built in the world for nearly a thousand years, until the completion of the Medieval Seville Cathedral in 1520.

The Hagia Sophia

The current building was originally constructed as a church between 532 and 537 AD on the orders of the Byzantine Emperor Justinian, and was in fact the third Church of the Holy Wisdom to occupy the site (the previous two had both been destroyed by riots). It was designed by two architects, Isidore of Miletus and Anthemius of Tralles. The Church contained a large collection of holy relics and featured, among other things, a 50 foot (15 m) silver iconostasis. It was the patriarchal church of the Patriarch of Constantinople and the religious focal point of the Eastern Orthodox Church for nearly 1000 years.

In 1453, Constantinople was conquered by the Ottoman Turks and Sultan Mehmed II ordered the building to be converted into a mosque. The bells, altar, iconostasis, and sacrificial vessels were removed, and many of the mosaics were eventually plastered over. The Islamic features - such as the mihrab, the minbar, and the four minarets outside - were added over the course of its history under the Ottomans. It remained as a mosque until 1935, when it was converted into a museum by the Republic of Turkey.

Hagia Sophia is one of the greatest surviving examples of Byzantine architecture. Of great artistic value was its decorated interior with mosaics and marble pillars and coverings. The vast interior has a complex structure. The vast nave is covered by a central dome which has a maximum diametre of 31.24 metres (102 ft 6 in) and a height from floor level of 55.6 metres (182 ft 5 in), about one fourth smaller than the dome of the Pantheon. The dome seems rendered weightless by the unbroken arcade of 40 arched windows under it, which help flood the colourful interior with light. Due to consecutive repairs in the course of its history, the dome has lost its perfect circular base and has become somewhat elliptical with a diametre varying between 31.24 m (102 ft 6 in) and 30.86 m (101 ft 3 in).

7

The Leaning Tower of Pisa

The Leaning Tower of Pisa or simply The Tower of Pisa is the campanile, or freestanding bell tower, of the cathedral of the Italian city of Pisa. It is situated behind the Cathedral and it is the third structure by time in Pisa's Piazza del Duomo. Although intended to stand vertically, the tower began leaning to the southeast soon after the onset of construction in 1173 due to a poorly laid foundation and loose substrate that has allowed the foundation to shift direction. The tower presently leans to the southwest.

The Leaning Tower of Pisa

The height of the tower is 55.86 m (183.27 ft) from the ground on the lowest side and 56.70 m (186.02 ft) on the highest side. The width of the walls at the base is 4.09 m (13.42 ft) and at the top 2.48 m (8.14 ft). Its weight is estimated at 14,500 tonnes. The tower has 296 or 294 steps; the seventh floor has two fewer steps on the north-facing staircase. The tower leans at an angle of 3.97 degrees. This means that the top of the tower is 3.9 metres from where it would stand if the tower were perfectly vertical.

The Tower of Pisa was a work of art, performed in three stages over a period of about 177 years. Construction of the first floor of the white marble campanile began on August 9, 1173. This first floor is surrounded by pillars with classical capitals, leaning against blind arches.

The tower began to sink after construction progressed to the third floor in 1178. This was due to a mere three-metre foundation, set in weak, unstable subsoil. This means the design was flawed from the beginning. Construction was subsequently halted for almost a century, because the Pisans were almost continually engaged in battles with Genoa, Lucca and Florence. This allowed time for the underlying soil to settle. Otherwise, the tower would almost certainly have toppled. In 1198, clocks were temporarily installed on the third floor of the unfinished construction.

In 1272, construction resumed under Giovanni di Simone, architect of the Camposanto. In an effort to compensate for the tilt, the engineers built higher floors with one side taller than the other. This made the tower begin to lean in the other direction. Because of this, the tower is actually curved. The seventh floor was completed in 1319. There are seven bells, one for each note of the musical scale. The largest one was installed in 1655.

The Seven Natural Wonders of the World

The world's natural wonders differ from the other grouping of wonders in that they were not made or improved upon by humans. They actually humble humanity.

The local native peoples have known these wonders for millenia, however this list came to the notice of the Western world relatively recently. For example, Mount Everest wasn't identified as the world's highest peak until 1852, and its exact height is periodically disputed to this day.

Today, these wonders have become places of pilgrimage, where awe is its own reward.

Mount Everest

Mount Everest, is the highest mountain on Earth, as measured by the height of its summit above sea level, which is 8,848 metres (29,029 feet). The mountain, which is part of the Himalaya range in High Asia, is located on the border between Sagarmatha Zone, Nepal, and Tibet, China.

Mount Everest

In 1856, the Great Trigonometric Survey of India established the first published height of Everest at 29,002 ft (8,840 m), although at the time Everest was known as Peak XV. In 1865, Everest was given its official English name by the Royal Geographical Society upon recommendation of Andrew Waugh, the British Surveyor General of India at the time. Waugh was unable to propose an established local name due to Nepal and Tibet being closed to foreigners at the time, although Chomolungma had been in common use by Tibetans for centuries.

The highest mountain in the world attracts climbers of all levels, from well experienced mountaineers to novice climbers willing to pay substantial sums to professional mountain guides to complete a successful climb. By the end of the 2007 climbing season, there had been 3,679 ascents to the summit by 2,436 individuals.

Everest has claimed 210 lives, including 15 who perished during a 1996 storm high on the mountain. Conditions are so difficult in the death zone that most corpses have been left where they fell, some of which are visible from standard climbing routes. In 1856, Andrew Waugh announced Everest (then known as Peak XV) as 29,002 feet (8,840 m) high, after several years of calculations based on observations made by the Great Trigonometric Survey.

More recently, the mountain has been found to be 8,848 metres (29,029 ft) high, although there is some variation in the measurements. On 9 October 2005, after several months of measurement and calculation, the PRC's State Bureau of Surveying and Mapping officially announced the height of Everest as 8,844.43 m ± 0.21 m (29,017.16 ± 0.69 ft). They claimed it was the most accurate and precise measurement to date. This height is based on the actual highest point of rock and not on the snow and ice covering it. The Chinese team also measured a snow/ice depth of 3.5 m, which is in agreement with a net elevation of 8,848 m. The snow and ice thickness varies over time, making a definitive height of the snow cap impossible to determine.

The Great Barrier Reef

The Great Barrier Reef is the world's largest coral reef system, composed of over 2,900 individual reefs and 900 islands stretching for 2,600 kilometres (1,600 mi) over an area of approximately 344,400 square kilometres (1.330 x 10 sq mi). The reef is located in the Coral Sea, off the coast of Queensland in northeast Australia.

The Great Barrier Reef

The Great Barrier Reef can be seen from outer space and is the world's biggest single structure made by living organisms. This reef structure is composed of and built by billions of tiny organisms, known as coral polyps. The Great Barrier Reef supports a wide diversity of life, and was selected as a World Heritage Site in 1981. CNN has labelled it one of the seven natural wonders of the world. The Queensland National Trust has named it a state icon of Queensland.

A large part of the reef is protected by the Great Barrier Reef Marine Park, which helps to limit the impact of human use, such as overfishing and tourism. Other environmental pressures to the reef and its ecosystem include water quality from runoff, climate change accompanied by mass coral bleaching, and cyclic outbreaks of the crown-of-thorns starfish. The Great Barrier Reef is a distinct physiographic province of the larger East Australian Cordillera division. It encompasses the smaller Murray Islands physiographic section.

According to the Great Barrier Reef Marine Park Authority, the current, living reef structure is believed to have begun growing on the older platform about 20,000 years ago. The Australian Institute of Marine Science agrees, which places the beginning of the growth of the current reef at the time of the Last Glacial Maximum. At around that time, the sea level was 120 metres (390 ft) lower than it is today.

The Great Barrier Reef World Heritage Area has been divided into 70 bioregions, of which 30 are reef bioregions, and 40 are non-reef bioregions. In the northern part of the Great Barrier Reef, ribbon reefs and deltaic reefs have formed; these structures are not found in the rest of the Great Barrier Reef system. There are no atolls in the system, and reefs attached to the mainland are rare. Thirty species of whales, dolphins, and porpoises have been recorded in the Great Barrier Reef, including the dwarf minke whale, Indo-Pacific humpback dolphin, and the humpback whale. Large populations of dugongs live there.

The Grand Canyon

The Grand Canyon is a steep-sided gorge carved by the Colorado River in the U.S. state of Arizona. It is largely contained within the Grand Canyon National Park - one of the first national parks in the United States.

The Grand Canyon

The longstanding scientific consensus has been that the canyon was created by the Colorado River over a period of six million years, but research released in 2008 suggests a much longer 17 million year time span. The canyon is 277 miles (446 km) long, ranges in width from 4 to 18 miles (6.4 to 29 km) and attains a depth of more than a mile (1.6 km). Nearly two billion years of the Earth's history have been exposed as the Colorado River and its tributaries cut their channels through layer after layer of rock while the Colorado Plateau was uplifted. The "canyon started from the west, then another formed from the east, and the two broke through and met as a single majestic rent in the earth some six million years ago. The merger apparently occurred where the river today, coming from the north, bends to the west, in the area known as the Kaibab Arch."

The Grand Canyon is a massive rift in the Colorado Plateau that exposes uplifted Proterozoic and Paleozoic strata and is also one of the six distinct physiographic sections of the Colorado Plateau province. The Grand Canyon is unmatched throughout the world for the vistas it offers to visitors on the rim. It is not the deepest canyon in the world - Cotahuasi Canyon (11598 feet or 3535 m) and Colca Canyon (10499 feet or 3200 m), both in Arequipa, Peru, and Hell's Canyon (7,993 feet or 2436 m) on the Oregon-Idaho border, are all deeper - but Grand Canyon is known for its overwhelming size and its intricate and colourful landscape. Geologically it is significant because of the thick sequence of ancient rocks that are beautifully preserved and exposed in the walls of the canyon. These rock layers record much of the early geologic history of the North American continent.

Uplift associated with mountain building events later moved these sediments thousands of feet upward and created the Colorado Plateau. The higher elevation has also resulted in greater precipitation in the Colorado River drainage area, but not enough to change the Grand Canyon area from being semi-arid.

Victoria Falls

The Victoria Falls or Mosi-oa-Tunya (the Smoke that Thunders) is a waterfall situated in southern Africa on the Zambezi River between the countries of Zambia and Zimbabwe. The falls are, by some measures, the largest waterfall in the world, as well as being among the most unusual in form, and having arguably the most diverse and easily seen wildlife of any major waterfall site.

Victoria Fall

Although Victoria Falls constitute neither the highest nor the widest waterfall in the world, the claim it is the largest is based on a width of 1.7 kilometres (1 mi) and height of 108 metres (360 ft), forming the largest sheet of falling water in the world. The falls' maximum flow rate compares well with that of other major waterfalls.

The unusual form of Victoria Falls enables virtually the whole width of the falls to be viewed face-on, at the same level as the top, from as close as 60 metres (200 ft), because the whole Zambezi River drops into a deep, narrow slotlike chasm, connected to a long series of gorges. Few other waterfalls allow such a close approach on foot. Many of Africa's animals and birds can be seen in the immediate vicinity of Victoria Falls, and the continent's range of river fish is also well represented in the Zambezi, enabling wildlife viewing and sport fishing to be combined with sightseeing.

For a considerable distance above the falls, the Zambezi flows over a level sheet of basalt, in a shallow valley bounded by low and distant sandstone hills. The river's course is dotted with numerous tree-covered islands, which increase in number as the river approaches the falls. There are no mountains, escarpments, or deep valleys which might be expected to create a waterfall, only flat plateau extending hundreds of kilometres in all directions.

The falls are formed as the full width of the river plummets in a single vertical drop into a chasm 60-120 metres (200-400 ft) wide, carved by its waters along a fracture zone in the basalt plateau. The depth of the chasm, called the First Gorge, varies from 80 metres (262 ft) at its western end to 108 metres (360 ft) in the centre. The only outlet to the First Gorge is a 110-metre-wide (360 ft) gap about two-thirds of the way across the width of the falls from the western end, through which the whole volume of the river pours into the Victoria Falls gorges.

The Harbour of Rio de Janeiro

At the beginning of the 16th century, the Portuguese explorers who sailed down Brazil's coast kept track of their discoveries, and the days of the year, by naming the former for the latter. On New Year's Day, 1502, they glided toward a narrow opening in the coastline, guarded by fabulously shaped mountains. Beyond this entrance lay a body of water stretching 20 miles inland. Convinced that they had reached the mouth of a great river, they named the area River of the First of January.

The Harbour of Rio de Janeiro

The large waterway was not a river; it was an island-studded bay that the Tamoio people had long before named Guanabara - "arm of the sea." Nearly five centuries later, both the native and European names persist. But now, instead of caravels and dugouts, supertankers and yachts glide across the magnificent balloon-shaped harbour of Guanabara Bay. No longer a tropical wilderness teeming with tapirs and jaguars, the bay's western shores now hold a roaring metropolis called Rio de Janeiro - the River of January.

The great bay that looked like a river was only one of many illusions that Rio held. Europeans called the smaller bay of Botafago, under Sugarloaf, a "lake"; the Tamoio themselves named Guanabara Bay's eastern edge Niteroi, meaning "hidden waters." For early European voyagers, it was as though, when Rio hove into view, the curtain rose on a stage set with such strange, striking shapes and forms that virtually everything looked like something else.

Guarding the entrance to the bay, the naked and lopsided mountain the Portuguese called Pao de Acucar evoked the sugarloaves fashioned on the island of Madeira. They called the highest mountain Corcovado - "the hunchback" - for its humped profile. Today, a statue of Christ the Redeemer crowns the 2,300-foot-high peak.

The bay's vastness has been shrinking. With usable land at a premium, landfill has twice altered Guanabara Bay's contours. In the 1920s and again in the 1960s, small hills that once had been home to Rio's earliest settlers were sluiced through pipes to create bayfill. The new land now anchors an airport, a six-lane highway, parkland and beaches, the city's modern art museum, and other 20th-century landmarks as Rio looks to its great bay for elbow room.

Paricutin Volcano

Paricutin is a cinder cone volcano in the Mexican state of Michoacan, close to a lava-covered village of the same name. It appears on many versions of the Seven Natural Wonders of the World. Paricutin is part the Michoacan-Guanajuato Volcanic Field, which covers much of west central Mexico.

Paricutin Volcano

The volcano began as a fissure in a cornfield owned by Tarascan farmer Dionisio Pulido on February 20, 1943. Pulido, his wife, and their son all witnessed the initial eruption of ash and stones first-hand as they plowed the field. Much of the volcano's growth occurred during its first year, while it was still in the explosive pyroclastic phase. Nearby villages Paricutin (after which the volcano was named) and San Juan Parangaricutiro were both buried in lava and ash; the residents relocated to a vacant land nearby.

At the end of this phase, after roughly one year, the volcano had grown 336 metres tall. For the next eight years the volcano would continue erupting, although this was dominated by relatively quiet eruptions of lava that would scorch the surrounding 25 km^2 of land. The volcano's activity would slowly decline during this period until the last six months of the eruption, during which violent and explosive activity was frequent. In 1952 the eruption ended and Paricutin went quiet, attaining a final height of 424 metres above the cornfield from which it was born. The volcano has been quiet since. Like most cinder der cones, Paricutin is which in is a monogenetic volcano, which means that it will never erupt again.

Volcanism is a common part of the Mexican landscape. Paricutin is merely the youngest of more than 1,400 volcanic vents that exist in the Trans-Mexican Volcanic Belt and North America. The volcano is unique in the sense that its formation was witnessed from its very conception. Three people died as a result of lightning strikes caused by the eruptions, but no deaths were attributed to the lava or asphyxiation.

There are actually two different elevations attributed to Paricutin. According to some sources, the elevation of the volcano is 3,170 metres (10,397 feet). Other sources, as well as many maps along with GPS measurements on Google Earth have the elevation of Paricutin at only 2,774 metres (9,101 feet).

The Northern Lights

Northern lights, or Aurora borealis brings together two mythological deities - Aurora, the Roman goddess of the dawn, and Boreas, Greek god of the north wind - to describe an event witnessed mostly at night in the high northerly latitudes. An identical phenomenon, the aurora australis, occurs in the high latitudes of the Southern Hemisphere, a region that has always been much more sparsely inhabited than the planet's northern reaches. Only a few eyewitness accounts of the aurora australis were available before 20th-century explorers arrived in Antarctica.

The Northern Lights

By contrast, the flowing ribbons, sky-filling swirls, otherworldly glow, gossamer veils, and brilliant rays of the aurora borealis are a regular presence that have awed and terrified northern peoples for thousands of years. To Finns the aurora was "fox fire" sparked by glistening fur. Some Alaskan Inuit saw the dancing souls of deer, seals, salmon, and beluga; others believed that if they whistled the lights might snatch them away. The Athabascan saw messages from their dead, the "sky dwellers."

For a long time, scientists offered almost as many interpretations of the northern lights as did the traditional peoples who observed them. The 20th century has brought with it studies of the earth's magnetism and the sun's workings. The aurora arises in the roiting turbulence of the sun. More than 100,000 times hotter than boiling water, the sun's interior chops the atoms that form solar gases into a thin stream of electrically charged particles - protons and electrons. Both matter and energy, this stream continuously erupts from the sun and is called the solar wind. Two or three days after bursting from the sun's surface at speeds of up to 500 miles a second, the solar wind reaches the earth, 93 million miles away.

The solar wind has the force to swiftly annihilate life on earth. What stops it from doing so is the shielding power of the planet's magnetic field, reaching out more than 40,000 miles into space. Like the earth, the sun is also a mighty magnet, and the solar wind carries fragments of its magnetic field. As solar particles crash into the planet's magnetic field, the fields repel each other.

Though most of the solar wind harmlessly sideswipes the magnetic shield, small streams of solar particles do manage to become trapped, spiraling down toward the planet's north and south magnetic poles. As they tumble, beams of electrons spread, ripple, and swirl, and yet their movements remain invisible. But when the solar wind hits the upper reaches of the ionosphere and encounters atmospheric gases, it starts churning the thin soup of oxygen and nitrogen there. Marvelous shapes and flowing patterns begin to appear. Electrons bouncing around among atoms of oxygen create a greenish glow much lower. Nitrogen molecules hit by solar wind may shine bright pink, or blue and violet, depending upon their distance from the surface.

The ever changing dance of lights belies the aurora's permanence. Though only parts of it can be seen at any time, and almost never during the day, the aurora borealis forms a 2,000-mile-wide auroral oval above the magnetic north pole day in and day out, year after year.

What can dramatically change the oval are the occasional spikes in solar activity that turn the solar wind into a raging hurricane. Then, for a few days, the auroral oval flows toward the Equator and treats sky-gazers as far south as Mexico to midnight extravaganzas. At the same time, electromagnetic disturbances intensify, with overloaded power lines and scrambled communications serving to remind us of the force behind the celestial fireworks.

The Seven Underwater Wonders of the World

A noted marine explorer named Jacques-Yves Cousteau wrote: *"It is all strange, unearthly, and yet familiar. Strange because the sea, once it casts its spell, holds one in its net of wonders forever."*

Diving is becoming a much more popular sport as humans become more fascinated with the diverse ecosystems of the deep. Coral reefs, like many of these underwater wonders, are structures built by living organisms. Second only to tropical rain forests in biodiversity, coral reefs provide homes for thousands of species. Unfortunately, they are at risk all around the world.

To promote awareness of the fragile marine ecosystem, CEDAM International - an organization dedicated to conservation, education, diving, and marine research - began the Seven Wonders of the World project in 1989. The message was simple: If underwater wonders are not protected, they will be lost forever. After considering sites around the world, CEDAM chose Palau, the Belize Barrier Reef, the Galapagos Islands, the Northern Red Sea, Lake Baikal, the Great Barrier Reef, and the Deep Sea Vents. Each was selected on the basis of its natural beauty, unique marine life, scientific research value, environmental significance, and whether it is representative of an overall area.

By focusing on these seven sites, CEDAM hopes to promote the protection of all underwater wonders. *"We are the first generation to explore the wonders of the underwater world,"* says George Page, host of the public television series Nature. *"Let's hope we are not the last."*

Palau

Palau (Palauan *Belau*), republic, W Pacific Ocean, comprises more than 300 islands, islets, and atolls of the Caroline group. Major islands include Koror, the current seat of government, and Babelthuap, the future capital. Area of the republic, 487 sq km (188 sq mi). Of the total population (1990, 15,122), ethnic Palauans make up about 83%; minority groups include Filipinos and Chinese. Palauan and English are the official languages. Leading occupations include fishing and subsistence agriculture; the country relies heavily on aid from the U.S. The U.S. dollar is the legal currency. Palau has a presidential system with a bicameral legislature.

Palau

Spain formally claimed the Palau Islands in 1885 but sold them to Germany 14 years later. Japan seized them in 1914 and established a naval base. The islands were captured by American forces in 1944, during World War II. After the war they became part of the Trust Territory of the Pacific Islands, administered by the U.S. under UN supervision. In 1980 the islands adopted a republican constitution. During the next ten years, a compact of free association granting Palau independence, but with defense remaining the responsibility of the U.S., was repeatedly submitted to referendum. The measure was supported by a majority of Palauan voters, but not by the 75 percent required to overcome a constitutional ban on port calls by U.S. nuclear-armed vessels. After a constitutional amendment eased this requirement, the compact passed in 1993. Palau became independent on Oct. 1, 1994, and was admitted to the UN in December.

The Belize Barrier Reef

The second largest barrier reef in the world rises from the seafloor off the coast of Belize. A diver's paradise, it is known for fascinating coral formations, myriad fish and invertebrates, and exceptional water clarity.

The Belize Barrier Reef

On the ocean side of this 160-mile-long reef is a popular tourist designation known as Lighthouse Reef. Here, crystal-clear waters fill the famous Blue Hole, a crater more than 1,000 feet across and just over 400 feet deep. At the surface, healthy coral formations rim this wonder within a wonder, but at a depth of 125 feet, neither corals nor fish can be found. Instead, a diver finds stalactites formed during the Ice Age, when the world sea level was much lower and the Blue Hole was a subterranean cavern. The hole formed when the cavern's roof collapsed.

To the south is Glover's Reef, surrounded by waters so clear that visibility even at night is quite good: The long shaft of a diver's torch can pierce the water to a distance of 15 feet. Because it is several miles from the mainland, this reef is not affected by silt and sediment runoff. At Glover's, the arrival of a diver startles bright red cardinalfish swimming in open water, they rely on organs called lateral lines running along both sides of their bodies. A combination of sonar and radar, a lateral line senses vibrations and movements in the water, allowing fish to detect predators and pray. It's also an early warning device. As a fish swims, it creates a sort of bow wake that bounces off solid objects. When another fish feels the wake, it moves to avoid a collision.

Glover's Reef is home to the Emerald Forest, a site named for magnificent elk horn coral "trees" having trunks a foot diametre and canopies more than ten feet high. Several kinds of exotic fish also live here, and at night, a camera-bearing diver can catch them asleep, tucked in against the reef, but still out in the open. Butterflyfish as colourful as backyard butterflies hover in the water. So do hogfish with pig like snouts, trumpetfish that look like two-foot-long musical instruments, and parrotfish, their beaklike mouths closed for the night.

Not all of the reef's creatures are lost in sleep, however. Manta rays and sharks prowl the darkness, seeking meals. Lobsters, crabs, shrimp, and nudibranchs (the beautiful slugs of the sea) search the reef for food and mates. A Nassau grouper gets its mouth "cleaned" by a tiny shrimp, which darts from side to side and from top to bottom to remove small parasites and dead flesh from the cooperative fish, its mouth frozen in a wide yawn. The shrimp gets a free meal, so to speak. Dr. Mary Wicksten, a marine biologist at Texas A&M University and a specialist in these so-called cleaning stations, says that fish seek out established stations on the reef because the activity is important for their health. Like several other reef fish, the Nassau grouper is remarkable for its ability to change sex as it gets older, increasing its chances for reproductive success when another grouper is met.

At a natural cut in Glover's Reef, where water surges during the changing of the tide, a diver can free-fall horizontally, whipped along by the strong current. But fish hover without obvious effort, their streamlined bodies designed by nature to keep them in place in such conditions. Jutting from the walls of the cut, like fingers on a huge hand, are lavender tube sponges that eat by filtering tiny plants and animals from the sea. Soft coral sea fans, also filter feeders, bend in the breeze like underwater current that brings them a constant supply of food. The dominant life-form here is the hard coral, which is capable of withstanding the force of very strong wave action.

Where the current exits this canyon, it stirs up sand from the floor of a lagoon, reducing visibility. Somewhere near the bottom, turtles and manatees leisurely feed on sea grasses, while small coral heads form mini-reefs alive with tiny fish.

Across the lagoon is the Hol Chan Marine Reserve, a small area off Ambergris Cay where the tangled roots of a mangrove forest reach into the water. Even here, small fish dart among the roots, looking for meals or protection from predators.

Hol Chan, which is Maya for "the cut," was established in 1987. It encompasses all three habitats of the barrier reef ecosystem: reef, lagoon, and mangroves. Although separate, each area depends on the others. Marine scientist Jacque Carter, who has long studied Belize's fish, writes: "The mangroves are a feeding and breeding ground for reef fishes; they also trap silt and sediment runoff before it reaches the reef. The lagoon is...a feeding ground for many reef fishes, and the sea grasses... trap reef-smothering particles [keeping them] from reaching the lagoon, mangroves and shore areas from destructive wave action. If one area is damaged, the others are also affected – which is why it is important to protect the entire system, and not just the beautiful coral reef."

The Galapagos Islands

Galápagos Islands or Colón Archipelago, group of islands, Ecuador, in the Pacific Ocean, constituting a province of the country, about 965 km (about 600 mi) off the W coast. The archipelago consists of six larger and numerous smaller islands lying on or near the equator. The principal islands are Isabela, San Cristóbal, Fernandina, San Salvador, Santa María, and Santa Cruz. The total land area is 8010 sq km (3093 sq mi).

The Galapagos Islands

The islands are volcanic in origin, with level shorelines and mountainous interiors culminating in high central craters, some of which rise more than 1520 m (5000 ft) above sea level. Several volcanoes are active. The islands are fringed with mangroves; farther inland, although still in coastal regions, where little rain falls, the vegetation consists chiefly of thorn trees, cactus, and mesquite. In the uplands, which are exposed to a heavy mist, the flora is more luxuriant. The climate and the temperature of the waters surrounding the islands are modified by the cold Humboldt Current from the Antarctic.

The Galápagos group is noted for its fauna, which includes numerous animals found only in the archipelago and different subspecies on separate islands. Unique to the archipelago are six species of giant tortoise (Span. *galápago*—thus the islands' name). Other reptiles on the islands include two species of large lizards of the iguana family: a burrowing land lizard and an unusual marine lizard that dives into the ocean for seaweed. The islands contain as many as 85 different species of birds, including flamingos, flightless cormorants, finches, and penguins. Sea lions are numerous, as are many different shore fish. Part of the Galápagos is a wildlife sanctuary.

The Northern Red Sea

The Red Sea is a salt water inlet of the Indian Ocean between Africa and Asia. The connection to the ocean is in the south through the Bab el Mandeb sound and the Gulf of Aden. In the north are the Sinai Peninsula, the Gulf of Aqaba, and the Gulf of Suez.

The Northern Red Sea

Occupying a part of the Great Rift Valley, the Red Sea has a surface area of about 438,000 km² (169,100 square miles). It is roughly 2250 km (1398 mi) long and, at its widest point at 355 km (220.6 miles) wide. It has a maximum depth of 2211 m (7254 ft) in the central median trench and an average depth of 490 m(1,608 feet), but there are also extensive shallow shelves, noted for their marine life and corals. The sea is the habitat of over 1,000 invertebrate species and 200 soft and hard corals and is the world's northernmost tropical sea.

The Red Sea lies between arid land, desert and semi-desert. The main reasons for the better development of reef systems along the Red Sea is because of its greater depths and an efficient water circulation pattern, The Red Sea water mass exchanges its water with the Arabian Sea, Indian Ocean via the Gulf of Aden. The Red Sea is one of the most saline water bodies in the world, due to the effects of the water circulation pattern, resulting from evaporation and wind stress. Salinity ranges between 3.6 and 3.8%.

The climate of the Red Sea is the result of two distinct monsoon seasons; a northeasterly monsoon and a southwesterly monsoon. Monsoon winds occur because of the differential heating between the land surface and sea. Very high surface temperatures coupled with high salinities makes this one of the hottest and saltiest bodies of seawater in the world. The average surface water temperature of the Red Sea during the summer is about 26 °C (79 °F) in the north and 30 °C (86 °F) in the south, with only about 2 °C (3.6 °F) variation during the winter months. The overall average water temperature is 22 °C (72 °F). The scarcity of rainfall and no major source of fresh water to the Red Sea result in the excess evaporation as high as 205 cm (81 in) per year and high salinity with minimal seasonal variation.

Lake Baikal

Lake Baikal is in Southern Siberia in Russia, located between Irkutsk Oblast to the northwest and the Buryat Republic to the southeast, near the city of Irkutsk. It is also known as the "Blue Eye of Siberia". It contains more water than all the North American Great Lakes combined.

Lake Baikal

At 1,637 metres (5,371 ft), Lake Baikal is the deepest lake in the world, and the largest freshwater lake in the world by volume, holding approximately twenty percent of the world's total surface fresh water. Like Lake Tanganyika, Lake Baikal was formed in an ancient rift valley and therefore is long and crescent-shaped with a surface area (31,500 km^2) less than half that of Lake Superior or Lake Victoria. Baikal is home to more than 1,700 species of plants and animals, two thirds of which can be found nowhere else in the world and was declared a UNESCO World Heritage Site in 1996.

At more than 25 million years old, it is the oldest lake in the world. While Lake Baikal was known as the "North Sea" in historical Chinese texts, it was situated in the then Xionu territory and very little was known about Lake Baikal until the Trans-Siberian railway was built between 1896 and 1902. The scenic loop encircling Lake Baikal needed 200 bridges and 33 tunnels. As this railway was being built, a large hydrogeographical expedition headed by F.K. Drizhenko produced the first detailed atlas of the contours of Baikal's depths. The atlas demonstrated that Lake Baikal has more water than all of North America's Great Lakes combined —23,600 cubic kilometres (5,662.4 cu mi), about one fifth of the total fresh water on the earth.

At 636 kilometres (395 mi) long and 79 kilometres (49 mi) wide, Lake Baikal has the largest surface area of any freshwater lake in Asia (31,494 km^2) and is the deepest lake in the world (1,637 metres, previously measured at 1,620 metres). The bottom of the lake is 1,285 metres below sea level, but below this lies some 7 kilometres (4.3 mi) of sediment, placing the rift floor some 8-9 kilometres (more than 5 miles) below the surface: the deepest continental rift on Earth. In geological terms, the rift is young and active—it widens about two centimetres per year. The fault zone is also seismically active: there are hot springs in the area and notable earthquakes every few years. It drains into the Angara tributary of the Yenisei.

The Great Barrier Reef

Great Barrier Reef looks almost like a wall of perpendicular rock rising out of the sea - only it is not rock; it is coral. The Great Barrier Reef lies underwater and has snared many ships, including **Captain Cook's** in 1770. Though being one of the world's longest natural wonders, it unfortunately is also the most fragile around. It is a sweeping 2,000 kms in length, spanning along the **northeast coast of Australia**. It covers an area of 344,000 square kms and is made up of the skeletons of marine polyps that lived and died there, so it is generally lime-based. Sometimes the Great Barrier Reef is as close as 50 kms to the coast.

The Great Barrier Reef

The Great Barrier Reef consists of more than 3000 reefs spanning from 1 hectare to 10,000 hectares in area and is mainly made up of coral. The reef, however, is not just about polyps - dead or alive - they are also large numbers of different forms of **marine life**. There are colourful and exotic fishes, countless shellfish and other fanciful creatures. It abounds in wildlife. The variety of marine life ranges from nearly microscopic fishes to that of the larger fishes like the whale and the sharks.

There are more than 1500 species of fish, 4000 types of mollusk and, because of the abundance of fish, the reef is also home to more than 200 species of birds. The Great Barrier Reef houses anything and everything that thrives in shallow warm water.

It is also the only collection of organisms visible from Earth's orbit. It was declared a **World Heritage** in 1981. However, conditions like pollution, climatic change and various forms of human intrusion severely threaten its survival and continuance.

7

The Deep Sea Vents

Deep-sea vents are also known as deepwater seeps, deep-sea springs, **hydro-thermal vents** and blacksmokers. Found at **ocean floor**, they are formed by volcanic and tectonic activity in areas where huge hostile plates are unite or spread apart. Magma erupts along the margins of these plates, usually slowly, but sometimes with such ferocity that it creates instant lava lakes.

The Deep Sea Vents

Black smokers were first discovered in 1977 around the Galápagos Islands by the National Oceanic and Atmospheric Administration by using a small submersible vehicle called Alvin which first took photographs of these vents. Today, black smokers are known to exist in the Atlantic and Pacific Oceans, at an average depth of 2100 metres.

Because no sunlight reaches the depths where the vents are found, these underwater wonders are visible only in the floodlights of a manned submersible. Pitch darkness, poison gas, heavy metals, extreme acidity, enormous pressure, frigid and searing water prevails at the deep seafloor which literally reminds us of hell.

Yet amazing communities of life exist at these vents and the inhabitants are perhaps the most fascinating of all the world's underwater wonders from a scientific perspective. Blind shrimp, giant white crabs, and a variety of tubeworms are just some of the more than 300 species of **vent organisms** that have been identified by biologists so far. The most striking fact is about the food chain that functions without sunlight. As it was believed earlier that only sunlight, through photosynthesis, could support life on Earth. But, at the vents, however, life begins with bacteria that metabolize hydrogen sulfide. The bacteria, in turn, become food for the other animals in the vent society.

One of the peculiar residents of these vents are the giant red-tipped tube worms-12-foot-tall creatures whose 300,000 tentacles strain food from the water. Equally fascinating residents include pink ventfish, **sea cucumbers**, sponges, and brittle stars, flowerlike animals that use their fine appendages to anchor themselves to rocks.

The Seven Wonders of the Modern World

The 20th century has provided spectacular advances in design, engineering, and construction which have allowed humanity to create an array of monumental structures. And from these, the American Society of Civil Engineers (ASCE), with help from experts around the world, selected these wonders: the Empire State building, the Itaipu Dam, the CN Tower, the Panama Canal, the Channel Tunnel, the North Sea Protection Works, and the Golden Gate Bridge.

These wonders embody an abundance of human ingenuity, thus showcasing humankind's ability to dream, plan, and achieve on a colossal, mind-boggling scale.

Man has an incredible ability to make the impossible, possible.

The Empire State Building

The Empire State Building is a 102-story Art Deco skyscraper in New York City at the intersection of Fifth Avenue and West 34th Street. Its name is derived from the nickname for the state of New York. It stood as the world's tallest building for more than forty years, from its completion in 1931 until construction of the World Trade Centre's North Tower was completed in 1972. Following the destruction of the World Trade Centre in 2001, the Empire State Building again became the tallest building in New York City.

The Empire State Building

The Empire State Building has been named by the American Society of Civil Engineers as one of the Seven Wonders of the Modern World. It was designated as a National Historic Landmark in 1986. In 2007, it was ranked number one on the List of America's Favourite Architecture according to the AIA.

Excavation of the site began on January 22, 1930, and construction on the building itself started symbolically on March 17 - St.Patrick's Day - per Al Smith's influence as Empire State, Inc. president. The project involved 3,400 workers, mostly immigrants from Europe, along with hundreds of Mohawk iron workers, many from the Kahnawake reserve near Montreal. According to official accounts, five workers died during the construction.

The Empire State Building rises to 1,250 feet (381 m) at the 102nd floor, and including the 203-foot (62 m) pinnacle, its full height reaches 1,453 feet (443 m) and (8 9/16th) inches (443 m). The building has 85 stories of commercial and office space representing 2,158,000 sq ft (200,500 m^2). It has an indoor and outdoor observation deck on the 86th floor. The remaining 16 stories represent the Art Deco tower, which is capped by a 102nd-floor observatory. Atop the tower is the 203-foot (62 m) pinnacle, much of which is covered by broadcast antennas, with a lightning rod at the very top.

The Empire State Building was the first building to have more than 100 floors. It has 6,500 windows and 73 elevators, and there are 1,860 steps from street level to the 102nd floor. It has a total floor area of 2,768,591 square feet (257,211 m^2); the base of the Empire State Building is about 2 acres (8,094 m^2). The building houses 1,000 businesses, and has its own zip code, 10118.

The Itaipu Dam

Itaipu is a hydroelectric dam on the Parana River located on the border between Brazil and Paraguay. The name "Itaipu" was taken from an isle that existed near the construction site. In the Guarani language, Itaipu means "the sound of a stone".

The Itaipu Dam

Itaipu Binacional is a company that runs the largest operational hydroelectric power plant in the world. It is a binational undertaking run by Brazil and Paraguay at the Parana River on the border section between the two countries, 15 km north of the Friendship Bridge. The project ranges from Foj do Iguacu, in Brazil, and Ciudad del Este in Paraguay, in the south to Guaira and Salto del Guaira in the north. The installed generation capacity of the plant is 14 GW, with 20 generating units of 700 MW each. In the year 2000, it achieved its generating record of 93.4 billion kilowatt-hours (kWh), which supplied 93% of the energy consumed by Paraguay and 20% of that consumed by Brazil as of 2005.

On May 5, 1984, the first generation unit started running in Itaipu. In 1994, the American Society of Civil Engineers elected the Itaipu Dam as one of the Seven Wonders of the Modern World.

In 1970, the consortium formed by the companies IECO (from the United States of America) and ELC (from Italy) the international competition for the realization of the viability studies and for the elaboration of the construction project. Work began in February 1971. On April 26, 1973, Brazil and Paraguay signed the Itaipu Treaty, the legal instrument for the hydroelectric exploitation of the Parana River by the two countries. On May 17, 1974, the Itaipu Binacional entity was created to administer the plant's construction. The works began in January of the following year. On October 14, 1978, the Parana River had its route changed, which allowed a section of the riverbed to dry so the dam could be built there.

The planes reservoir began its formation on October 13, 1982, when the dam works were completed and the side canal's gates were closed. Throughout this period, water rose 100 metres (330 ft) and reached the gates of the spillway at 10:00 AM on October 27 due to the heavy rains and flooding that took place at the time.

The CN Tower

The CN Tower, located in downtown Toronto, Ontario, Canada, is a communications and tourist tower standing 553.33 metres (1,815.39 ft) tall. It surpassed the height of the Ostankino Tower while still under construction in 1975, becoming the tallest freestanding structure on land in the world. On September 12, 2007, after holding the record for 31 years, the CN tower was surpassed in height by the still under-construction Burj Dubai. It remains the tallest freestanding structure in the Americas and the signature icon of Toronto's skyline, attracting more than two million international visitors annually.

The CN Tower

CN originally referred to Canadian National, the railway company that built the tower. Following the railway's decision to divest non-core freight railway assets, prior to the company's privatization in 1995 it transferred the tower to the Canada Lands Company, a federal Crown corporation responsible for real estate development.

The CN Tower consists of several substructures. The main portion of the tower is a hollow concrete hexagonal pillar containing the six elevators, stairwells, and power and plumbing connections. On top of this is a 102 metres (334.6 ft) metal broadcast antenna, carrying TV and radio signals. In 1995, the CN Tower was declared one of the modem Seven Wonders of the World by the American Society of Civil Engineers. It also belongs to the World Federation of Great Towers.

Construction on the CN Tower began on February 6, 1973 with massive excavations at the tower base for the foundation. By the time the foundation was complete, 56,000 tonnes (61,729 short tons) of dirt and shale were removed to a depth of 15 metres (49.2 ft) in the centre, and a base incorporating 7,000 cubic metres (9,156 cu yd) of concrete with 450 tonnes (496 short tons) of rebar and 36 tonnes (40 short tons) of steel cable had been built to a thickness of 6.7 metres (22 ft).

To build the main support pillar, a hydraulically-raised slipform was built at the base. This was a fairly impressive engineering feat on its own, consisting of a large metal platform that raised itself on jacks at about 6 metres (19.7 ft) per day as the concrete below set. Concrete was poured continuously by a team of 1,532 people until February 22, 1974, during which it had already become the tallest structure in Canada, surpassing the recently built Inco Superstack, which was built using similar methods.

The Panama Canal

The Panama Canal is a man-made canal in Panama which joins the Pacific and Atlantic oceans. One of the largest and most difficult engineering projects ever undertaken, it had an enormous impact on shipping between the two oceans, replacing the long and treacherous route via the Drake Passage and Cape Horn at the southernmost tip of South America. A ship sailing from New York to San Francisco via the canal travels 9,500 km (6,000 miles), well under half the 22,500 km (14,000 mi) route around Cape Horn.

The Panama Canal

The first attempt to construct a canal began in 1880 under French leadership. After this attempt failed and saw 21,900 workers die, the project of building a canal was attempted and completed by the United States in the early 1900s, with the canal opening in 1914. By the time the canal was completed, a total of 27,500 workmen are estimated to have died in the French and American efforts.

An all-water route between the oceans was still seen as the ideal solution, and the idea of a canal was enhanced by the success of the Suez Canal. The French, under Ferdinand de Lesseps, began construction on a sea-level canal (i.e., without locks) through what was then Colombia's province of Panama, on January 1, 1880. The French began work in a rush with insufficient prior study of the geology and hydrology of the region. Disease, particularly malaria and yellow fever, sickened and killed vast numbers of employees, ranging from labourers to top directors of the French company. Public health measures were ineffective because the role of the mosquito as a disease vector was then unknown.

These conditions made it impossible to maintain an experienced work force as fearful technical employees quickly returned to France. Even the hospitals contributed to the problem, unwittingly providing breeding places for mosquitoes inside the unscreened wards. Actual conditions were hushed-up in France to avoid recruitment problems. In 1893, after a great deal of work, the French scheme was abandoned due to disease and the sheer difficulty of building a sea-level canal, as well as lack of French field experience, such as downpours causing steel equipment to rust. The high toll from disease was one of the major factors in the failure; as many as 22,000 workers are estimated to have died during the main period of French construction (1881-1889).

5

The Channel Tunnel

The Channel Tunnel, also known as Channel or Eurotunnel, is a 50.5-kilometre (31.4 mi) undersea rail tunnel linking the United Kingdom and France, running beneath the English Channel at the Strait of Dover, connecting Folkestone, Kent in England to Coquelles near Calais in northern France. It is the second longest undersea tunnel in the world (after Japan's Seikan Tunnel).

Channel Tunnel

The tunnel carries high-speed Euro star passenger railway services, Euro tunnel Shuttle RORO vehicle transport and international rail freight trains. In 1996 the American Society of Civil Engineers identified the tunnel as one of the Seven Wonders of the Modern World.

Ideas for a cross-Channel fixed link existed as early as 1802 but the eventual successful project, organised by Eurotunnel, began construction in 1988. By 1994 the tunnel commenced operating its through-rail passenger services, linking London to Paris and Brussels, through-rail freight services and vehicle shuttle services. The project's cost overran predictions by 80%, and concessionaire Euro tunnel overestimated tunnel traffic and has met financial difficulty.

A small two-inch (5-cm) diametre pilot hole allowed the service tunnel to break through without ceremony on 30 October 1990. On 1 December 1990 Englishman Graham Fagg and Frenchman Phillipe Cozette broke through the service tunnel with the media watching. Eurotunnel completed the tunnel on time, and the tunnel was officially opened by Queen Elizabeth II and French President Francois Mitterrand in a ceremony held in Calais on 6 May 1994. The Queen travelled through the tunnel to Calais on a Eurostar train which stopped nose to nose with the train which carried President Mitterrand from Paris. Following the ceremony President Mitterrand and the Queen travelled on Le Shuttle to a similar ceremony in Folkestone.

The Channel Tunnel Rail Link (CTRL), now called High Speed 1, runs 69 miles (111 km) from St Pancras railway station in London to the Channel Tunnel portal at Folkestone in Kent. It cost £5.8 billion. On September 16, 2003 UK Prime Minister Tony Blair opened the first section of High Speed 1, from Folkestone to north Kent. On 6 November 2007 the Queen officially opened High Speed 1 and St Pancras International station, replacing the original slow link to Waterloo International railway station. On the completed High Speed 1, trains travel at 300 km/h (186 mph). The Eurostar journey from London to Paris takes 2 hours 15 minutes and London to Brussels takes 1 hour 51 minutes.

The North Sea Protection Works (Netherlands)

Unique in the world, this vast and complex system of dams, floodgates, storm surge barriers and other engineered works literally allows the Netherlands to exist. For centuries, the people of the Netherlands have repeatedly attempted to push back the sea -- only to watch merciless storm surges flood their efforts, since the nation sits below sea level and its land mass is still sinking. The North Sea Protection Works consists of two monumental steps the Dutch took to win their struggle to hold back the sea. Step One -- a 19-mile-long enclosure dam built between 1927 and 1932. The immense dike, 100 yards thick at the waterline, collars the neck of the estuary once known as the Zuiderzee. Step Two was the Delta Project to control the treacherous area where the mouths of the Meuse and Rhine Rivers break into a delta. The crowning touch was the Eastern Schelde Barrier, a two-mile barrier of tell gates slung between massive concrete piers. The gates fall only when storm-waters threaten. The North Sea Protection Works exemplifies humanity's ability to exist side-by-side with the forces of nature.

The North Sea Protection Works (Netherlands)

The Golden Gate Bridge

The Golden Gate Bridge is a suspension bridge spanning the Golden Gate, the opening of the San Francisco Bay onto the Pacific Ocean. As part of both US Highway 101 and California Route 1, it connects the city of San Francisco on the northern tip of the San Francisco Peninsula to Marin County.

The Golden Gate Bridge

The Golden Gate Bridge had the longest suspension bridge span in the world when it was completed in 1937 and has become an internationally recognized symbol of San Francisco and California.

Since its completion, the span length has been surpassed by eight other bridges. It still has the second longest suspension bridge main span in the United States, after the Verrazano-Narrows Bridge in New York City.

The Golden Gate Bridge spans the Golden Gate, a narrow, 400-foot (120 m) deep strait that serves as the mouth of the San Francisco Bay, between San Francisco at the northernmost tip of the San Francisco Peninsula, and the Marin Headlands at the far southern end of Marin County.

Although close by proximity, the two sides of the strait are separated by significant natural obstacles. Crossing the strait directly by boat is dangerous because of strong currents and lack of suitable landings. Ocean tides drive an average of 528 billion gallons (2 billion cubic metres) of water every six hours, at peak currents exceeding 5.6 miles per hour (2.5 m/s). The bridge has approximately 1,200,000 total rivets.

As the only road to exit San Francisco to the north, the bridge is part of both U.S. Route 101 and State Route 1 and on an average day 120,000 vehicles cross the bridge. The bridge has six total lanes of vehicle traffic, and walkways on both sides of the bridge. The median markers between the lanes are moved to conform to traffic patterns. On weekday mornings, traffic flows mostly southbound into the city, so four of the six lanes run southbound. Conversely, on weekday afternoons, four lanes run northbound. While there has been discussion concerning the installation of a movable barrier since the 1980s, the Bridge Board of Directors, in March 2005, committed to finding funding to complete the $2 million study required prior to the installation of a moveable median barrier. The eastern walkway is for pedestrians and bicycles during the weekdays and during daylight hours only, and the western walkway is open to bicyclists on weekday afternoons, weekends, and holidays.

Seven Forgotten Natural Wonders of the World

The **creations of nature** have always remained a mystery to the mankind. It is really beyond the perception and comprehension of human mind how Supreme Nature has continued with its miraculous creations! Nature sometimes seems to be an invisible artist or painter who paints magnificent landscapes with one stroke of his brush; these landscapes are either vibrant with colours or are brown, grey and dark with rugged and ravaged features. Sometimes Nature seems to be at its peculiar fancy -playing the role of a creator or destroyer- inventing and devastating at his omnipotent will.

The list of **seven forgotten natural wonders** includes those majestic creations of nature which have inspired awe and admiration of human minds in the recent past.

Angel Falls

Angel Falls is the world's highest free-falling waterfall at 979 m (3,212 ft), with a clear drop of 807 m (2,647 ft). It is located in the Canaima National Park, in the Gran Sabana region of Bolivar State, Venezuela. The height of the falls is so great that before getting anywhere near the ground, the water is buffeted by the strong winds and turned into mist.

Angel Falls

The base of the falls feeds into the Kerep river (alternately known as the Rio Gauya) which flows into the Churun River, a tributary of the Carrao River. In the indigenous Pemon language Angel Falls is called Kerepakupai meru meaning "waterfall of the deepest place".

Sir Walter Raleigh is sometimes said to have discovered Angel Falls, but these claims are considered "far-fetched". They were sighted in 1912 by the Venezuelan explorer Ernesto Sanchez La Cruz, but he did not publicize his discovery. They were not known to the outside world until the American aviator James "Jimmie" Crawford Angel flew over them on 16 November 1933 on a flight while he was searching for a valuable ore bed.

Returning on 9 October 1937, Angel tried to land his Flamingo monoplane "El Rio Caroni" atop Auyan-tepui but the plane was damaged when the wheels sunk into the marshy ground and he and his three companions, including his wife Marie, were forced to descend the tepui on foot. It took them 11 days to make their way back to civilization but news of their adventure spread and the waterfall was named 'Angel Falls" in his honour.

Angel's plane remained on top of the tepuy for 33 years before being lifted out by helicopter. The first recorded human to reach the river that feeds the falls was the Latvian explorer Aleksandrs Laime, also known as Alejandro Laime to the native Pemon tribe. He made the ascent of Auyan-tepui in 1955. He also reached Angel's plane on the same trip, 18 years after the crash landing. He gave the name of the river after one of the most beautiful rivers in Latvia, the river Gauja. While the indigenous name of the falls is rarely used anymore, the Pemon given name of the river, Kerep, is still widely used.

The Bay of Fundy

Bay of Fundy, large tidal inlet of the North Atlantic Ocean, separating the provinces of New Brunswick and Nova Scotia, and bordering on SE Maine. It is about 275 km (about 171 mi) long and up to 80 km (about 50 mi) wide. In the E, Fundy divides into two arms, Chignecto Bay on the N and Minas Channel (which leads into Minas Basin) on the S. The funnel effect of these narrowing arms increases the tidal range of the bay, and at times the water in the arms rises by as much as 18 m (about 60 ft), creating one of the world's highest tides. The tidal surge in Chignecto Bay produces a large crested wave, or bore, ranging to 1.8 m (about 6 ft) in height, in the lower Petitcodiac R. The rising tide in Fundy proper creates a "reversing falls" on the lower Saint John R., at Saint John, N.B. Passamaquoddy Bay, a W arm of Fundy, forms part of the boundary between New Brunswick and Maine. Although Fundy is very deep, navigation is difficult because of the rapid rise and fall of the tide. Major deepwater harbours are located at St. John and at Digby and Hantsport, N.S. Fundy National Park borders the bay in New Brunswick. The bay was discovered by the French explorer Pierre du Guast, sieur de Monts, in 1604.

The Bay of Fundy

Iguazu Falls

Iguazu Falls, Iguassu Falls, or Iguacu Falls are waterfalls of the Iguazu River located on the border of the Brazilian state of Parana and the Argentine province of Misiones. The falls divide the river into the upper and lower Iguazu.

Iguazu Falls

Legend has it that a god planned to marry a beautiful aborigine named Nalpi, who fled with her mortal lover Taroba in a canoe. In rage, the god sliced the river creating the waterfalls, condemning the lovers to an eternal fall. The first European to find the falls was the Spanish Conquistador Alvar Nunez Cabeza de Vaca in 1541, after whom one of the falls in the Argentine side is named.

The falls were rediscovered by Boselli at the end of the nineteenth century, and one of the Argentinian falls is named after him. The waterfall system consists of 275 falls along 2.7 kilometres (1.67 miles) of the Iguazu River.

Some of the individual falls are up to 82 metres (269 ft) in height, though the majority are about 64 metres (210 ft).

The Garganta del Diablo (Devil's Throat in English), a U-shaped 150-metre-wide and 700-metre-long (490 by 2300 feet) cliff, is the most impressive of all, and marks the border between Argentina and Brazil. Two thirds of the falls are within Argentine territory. About 900 metres of the 2.7-kilometre length does not have water flowing over it. The edge of the basalt cap recedes only 3 mm per year.

The water falling over Iguazu in peak flow has a surface area of about 40 ha (1.3 million ft^2) whilst Victoria in peak flow has a surface area of over 55 ha (1.8 million ft^2). By comparison, Niagara has a surface area of under 18.3 ha (600,000 ft^2). Victoria's annual peak flow is also greater than Iguazu's annual peak-9100 m^3/s versus 6500—though in times of extreme flood the two have recorded very similar maximum water discharge (well in excess of 12000 m^3/s). Niagara's annual peak flow is about 2800 m^3/s, although an all-time peak of 6800 has been recorded. Iguazu and Victoria fluctuate more greatly in their flow rate. Mist rises between 30 and 150 m (100 and 500 ft) from Iguazu's Garganta do Diabo, and over 300 in (1,000 ft) above Victoria (sometimes over 600 m).

Krakatoa Island

Krakatoa (Indonesian name: Krakatau, Portuguese name: Krakatao) is a volcanic island in the Sunda Strait between Java and Sumatra in **Indonesia.** It has erupted repetitively massively and with devastating consequences throughout recorded history. The best known eruption occurred in a chain of huge explosions on August 26-27, 1883. Several years of regional seismicity resulted in the famous caldera-forming eruption of August 1883.

Krakatoa Island

The 1883 eruption threw away more than 25 cubic kilometres of rock, ash, and pumice and generated the loudest sound ever historically reported - the cataclysmic explosion was distinctly heard as far away as Perth in Australia. Near Krakatoa, according to estimated records, 165 villages and towns were ruined and 132 seriously damaged, at least 36,417 people died, and many thousands were injured by the eruption, mostly in the tsunamis which followed the explosion. The eruption produced erratic weather and spectacular sunsets throughout the world for many months afterwards, as a result of sunlight reflected from suspended dust particles ejected by the volcano high into Earth's atmosphere. It has been described as one of the deadliest eruptions of the world.

Recent eruptions of **Krakatoa** have been at Anak Krakatau, an island that emerged in 1927. One tourist was killed and five more injured by an explosion at Anak Krakatau in 1993. Anak Krakatau is undergoing relatively dormant periods, lasting at least a couple days, punctuated by periods of nearly continuous eruption. After having 44 years rest, the child of Krakatoa appeared in December 1927 and it is expanding until now. Now the child of Krakatoa has reached approximately 200 m above sea level with the diametre of 2 kilometres.

The way to reach there is from Canti located in Kalianda. After about an hour's driving from Bandar Lampung, the boats take the tourists to the Krakatoa area.

Ancient Krakatoa was estimated 2,000 metres in height and radius of 9 kms.

Its great eruption happened in pre history in 416 as documented in the ancient Javanese book "Pustaka Raja", and left 3 islands safe i.e. Rakata, Sertung and Panjang Islands.

Mount Fuji of Japan

Fuji or Fujiyama, also Fuji-no-Yama or Fujisan, is in Japan, S Honshu Island, near Tokyo. Fuji, the celebrated sacred volcano and the highest mountain in Japan, rises as a cone to a height of 3776 m (12,389 ft) above sea level, with the apex broken by a cone-shaped crater 610 m (2000 ft) in diametre. The S slopes extend to the shore of Suruga Bay, and the isolated peak can be seen from many of the outlying prefectures. The mountain is part of Fuji-Hakone-Izu National Park. According to legend, Fuji arose from the plain during a single night in 286 BC. The most recent recorded eruption of Fuji lasted from Nov. 24, 1707, until Jan. 22, 1708. As the sacred mountain of Japan, it is visited annually by thousands of pilgrims from all parts of the country, and numerous shrines and temples are on its slopes. Fuji is also revered in Japanese literature and art.

Mount Fuji of Japan

Mount Kilimanjaro

Kilimanjaro, the highest mountain in Africa, located in northeastern Tanzania, near the border with Kenya. Kilimanjaro is a dormant volcano. Its two peaks stand 11 km (7 mi) apart and are connected by a broad ridge. Kibo, the higher peak, rises to 5,895 m (19,341 ft) above sea level, and the summit of Mawensi is 5,149 m (16,893 ft) above sea level. Although Kilimanjaro lies 3° south of the equator, an ice cap covers the crater of Kibo year-round; this ice cap is pierced by several small craters. "The Snows of Kilimanjaro" (1938), one of the most famous stories of American writer Ernest Hemingway, is set in the region. Kilimanjaro has a number of different vegetation zones on its steep slopes. Coffee and plantains are grown on the lower slopes of Kilimanjaro. The mountain was successfully scaled for the first time in 1889 by German geographer Hans Meyer and Austrian mountain climber Ludwig Purtscheller.

Mount Kilimanjaro

7

Niagara Falls

Niagara Falls are massive waterfalls on the Niagara River, straddling the international border separating the Canadian province of Ontario and the U.S. state of New York. The falls are 17 miles (27 km) north-northwest of Buffalo, New York, 75 miles (120 km) south-southeast of Toronto, Ontario, between the twin cities of Niagara Falls, Ontario, and Niagara Falls, New York.

Niagara Falls

Niagara Falls is composed of two major sections separated by Goat Island: Horseshoe Falls, on the Canadian side of the border and American Falls on the United States side. The smaller Bridal Veil Falls also is located on the American side, separated from the main falls by Luna Island. Niagara Falls were formed when glaciers receded at the end of the Wisconsin glaciation (the last ice age), and water from the newly-formed Great Lakes carved a path through the Niagara Escarpment en route to the Atlantic Ocean. While not exceptionally high, the Niagara Falls are very wide. More than six million cubic feet (168,000 m^3) of water fall over the crest line every minute in high flow, and almost 4 million cubic feet (110,000 m³) on average. It is the most powerful waterfall in North America.

Niagara Falls is divided into the Horseshoe Falls and the American Falls. The Horseshoe Falls drop about 173 feet (53 m), the height of the American Falls varies between 70-100 feet (21 m) because of the presence of giant boulders at its base. The larger Horseshoe Falls are about 2,600 feet (792 m) wide, while the American Falls are 1,060 feet (323 m) wide. The volume of water approaching the falls during peak flow season is 202,000 cubic feet per second (5,720 m³/s).

By comparison Africa's spectacular Victoria Falls has over 15 million cubic feet (424,750 m³) of water falling over its crest line each minute during the peak of the wet season (250,000 cu ft/7,079 m³ per second). Since the flow is a direct function of the Lake Erie water elevation, it typically peaks in late spring or early summer. During the summer months, 100,000 cubic feet per second (2,832 m³/s) of water actually traverses the Falls. The most complete views of Niagara Falls are available from the Canadian shoreline.

The Seven Forgotten Modern Wonders of the World

The Seven forgotten modern wonders of the world account for the brilliance of the human mind, its perceptive power and adroit endeavors, which were considered as some of the **greatest wonders of the world**, but not great enough to leave behind an indelible impression on humanity's mind, and lost to the other greater and stupendous works of the human imagination. The **momentous works** of art and architecture by the humans and their ability to capture in realistic frame baffled travellers and onlookers from times immemorial and with the advance of the science and technology, engineering skills and **construction facilities**, the human hands began to carve out of their minds, edifices which made the world pleasanter and beautiful. The Seven forgotten modern wonders of the world are part of such grand endeavors, and although somewhere lost from the minds of humans, are unique and intriguing in their own special ways.

The Clock Tower (Big Ben)

Big Ben tower clock famous for its accuracy and for its massive bell (weighing more than 13 tons). It is housed in St. Stephen's Tower, at the northern end of the Houses of Parliament, in the London borough of Westminster. In coordination with the Royal Greenwich Observatory, the chimes of Big Ben have been broadcast as a feature of the BBC's daily time signal since 1924, with brief interruptions (owing to repairwork) in 1934 and 1956. The clock was designed by Edmund Beckett Denison and built by E.J. Dent and, later, Frederick Dent. The name of the clock is said by some historians to stand for Sir Benjamin Hall, the commissioner of

The Clock Tower (Big Ben)

works. At the time of the clock and bell's installation in 1859, the name applied only to the bell, but it eventually came to indicate the clock itself. In 1956 the clock mechanism was restored and repaired. The hands of the clock are 9 and 14 feet (2.7 and 4.3 metres) long, respectively, and the clock tower rises to 320 feet (98 metres). The bell was cast by George Mears of Whitechapel and pulled to the tower by a wagon team of 16 horses. Shortly after it was installed, it developed a crack and was kept out of service until its repair in 1862.St. Stephen's Tower once contained a prison cell where "rioters" were confined. The leader of the woman suffrage movement, Emmeline Pankhurst, was placed in the cell in 1902 after demonstrating nearby.

The Eiffel Tower

The Eiffel Tower is an iron tower built on the Champ de Mars beside the Seine River in Paris. The tower has become a global icon of France and is one of the most recognizable structures in the world.

The Eiffel Tower

Named after its designer, engineer Gustave Eiffel, the Eiffel Tower is the tallest building in Paris and one of the most recognized structures in the world. More than 200,000,000 have visited the tower since its construction in 1889, including 6,719,200 in 2006, making it the most visited paid monument in the world. Including the 24 m (79 ft) antenna, the structure is 325 m (1,063 ft) high (since 2000), which is equivalent to about 81 levels in a conventional building.

The metal structure of the Eiffel Tower weighs 7,300 tonnes while the entire structure including non-metal components is approximately 10,000 tonnes. Depending on the ambient temperature, the top of the tower may shift away from the sun by up to 18 cm (7 in) because of thermal expansion of the metal on the side facing the sun. The tower also sways 6-7 cm (2-3 in) in the wind. The tower has a mass less than the mass of the air contained in a cylinder of the same dimensions that is 324 metres high and 88.3 metres in radius. The weight of the tower is 10,100 tonnes compared to 10,265 tonnes of air.

The first and second levels are accessible by stairways and lifts. At the first platform the stairs continue up from the east tower and the third level summit is only accessible by lift. From the first or second platform the stairs are open for anyone to ascend or descend regardless of whether they have purchased a lift ticket or stair ticket. The actual count of stairs includes 9 steps to the ticket booth at the base, 328 steps to the first level, 340 steps to the second level and 18 steps to the lift platform on the second level. When exiting the lift at the third level there are 15 more steps to ascend to the upper observation platform. The step count is printed periodically on the side of the stairs to give an indication of progress of ascent. The majority of the ascent allows for an unhindered view of the area directly beneath and around the tower although some short stretches of the stairway are enclosed.

The Gateway Arch

The Gateway Arch, also known as the Gateway to the West, is an integral part of the Jefferson National Expansion Memorial and the iconic image of St. Louis, Missouri. It was designed by Finnish-American architect Eero Saarinen and structural engineer Hannskarl Bandel. It stands 630 feet (192 m) tall, and is 630 feet (192 m) wide at its base, making it the tallest monument in the United States.

The Gateway Arch

The cross-sections of its legs are equilateral triangles, narrowing from 54 feet (16.5 m) per side at the base to 17 feet (5.2 m) at the top. Each wall consists of a stainless steel skin covering reinforced concrete from ground level to 300 feet (91 m), with carbon steel and bar from 300 feet (91 m) to the peak. The interior of the Arch is hollow and contains a unique transport system leading to an observation deck at the top. The interior of the Arch also contains two emergency stairwells of 1076 steps each, in the event of a need to evacuate the Arch or if a problem develops with the tram system.

The base of each leg at ground level had an engineering tolerance of one sixty-fourth of an inch or the two legs would not meet at the top. During construction, both legs were built up simultaneously. When the time came to connect both legs together at the apex, thermal expansion of the sunward facing south leg, prevented it from aligning precisely with the north leg. This alignment problem was solved when the Saint Louis City Fire Department sprayed the south leg with water from firehoses until it had cooled to the point where it aligned with the north leg. It is the tallest habitable structure in St. Louis (taller than One Metropolitan Square, the tallest building), and the second tallest in Missouri (behind One Kansas City Place in Kansas City).

Near the top of the arch, the rider exits the compartment and climbs a slight grade to enter the arched observation area. Small windows, almost invisible from the ground, allow views across the Mississippi River and southern Illinois with its prominent Mississippian culture mounds to the east at Cahokia, and the City of Saint Louis and St. Louis County to the west beyond the city. On a clear day, one can see up to thirty miles (48 km).

The Aswan High Dam

Arabic As-Sadd al-'Ali, rock-fill dam across the Nile River, at Aswan, Egypt, completed in 1970 (and formally inaugurated in January 1971) at a cost of about $1 billion. The dam, 364 feet (111 m) high, with a crest length of 12,562 feet (3,830 m) and a volume of 57,940,000 cubic yards (44,300,000 cubic m), impounds a reservoir, Lake Nasser, that has a gross capacity of 5.97 trillion cubic feet (169 billion cubic m). Of the Nile's total annual discharge, some 2.6 trillion cubic feet (74 billion cubic m) of water have been allocated by treaty between Egypt and The Sudan, with about 1.96 trillion cubic feet (55.5 billion cubic m) apportioned to Egypt and the remainder to The Sudan. Lake Nasser backs up

The Aswan High Dam

the Nile about 200 miles (320 km) in Egypt and almost 100 miles (160 km) farther upstream (south) in The Sudan; creation of the reservoir necessitated the costly relocation of the ancient Egyptian temple complex of Abu Simbel, which would otherwise have been submerged. Ninety thousand Egyptian fellahin (peasants) and Sudanese Nubian nomads had to be relocated. Fifty thousand Egyptians were transported to the Kawm Umbu valley, 30 miles (50 km) north of Aswan, to form a new agricultural zone called Nubaria; most of the Sudanese were resettled around Khashm al-Qirbah, Sudan. The Aswan High Dam yields enormous benefits to the economy of Egypt. For the first time in history, the annual Nile flood can be controlled by man. The dam impounds the floodwaters, releasing them when needed to maximize their utility on irrigated land, to water hundreds of thousands of new acres, to improve navigation both above and below Aswan, and to generate enormous amounts of electric power (the dam's 12 turbines can generate 10 billion kilowatt-hours annually). The reservoir, which has a depth of 300 feet (90 m) and averages 14 miles (22 km) in width, supports a fishing industry.The Aswan High Dam has produced several negative side effects, however, chief of which is a gradual decrease in the fertility and hence the productivity of Egypt's riverside agricultural lands. This is because of the dam's complete control of the Nile's annual flooding. Much of the flood and its load of rich fertilizing silt is now impounded in reservoirs and canals; the silt is thus no longer deposited by the Nile's rising waters on farmlands. Egypt's annual application of about 1 million tons of artificial fertilizers is an inadequate substitute for the 40 million tons of silt formerly deposited annually by the Nile flood.Completed in 1902, with its crest raised in 1912 and 1933, an earlier dam 4 miles (6 km) downstream from the Aswan High Dam holds back about 174.2 billion cubic feet (4.9 billion cubic m) of water from the tail of the Nile flood in the late autumn. Once one of the largest dams in the world, it is 7,027 feet (2,142 m) long and is pierced by 180 sluices that formerly passed the whole Nile flood, with its heavy load of silt.

The Hoover Dam

Hoover Dam, also known as Boulder Dam, is a concrete arch-gravity dam in the Black Canyon of the Colorado River, on the border between the U.S. states of Arizona and Nevada. When completed in 1935, it was both the world's largest electric power producing facility and the world's largest concrete structure.

The Hoover Dam

The dam, located 30 miles (48 km) southeast of Las Vegas, is named after Herbert Hoover, who played an instrumental role in its construction, first as Secretary of Commerce and then later as President of the United States. Construction began in 1931 and was completed in 1935, more than two years ahead of schedule.

To protect the construction site from flooding, two cofferdams were constructed. Construction of the upper cofferdam began in September 1932, even though the river had not yet been diverted.

A temporary horseshoe-shaped dike protected the cofferdam on the Nevada side of the river. After the Arizona tunnels were completed, and the river diverted, the work was completed much faster. Once the coffer dams were in place and the construction site dewatered, excavation for the dam foundation began. For the dam to rest on solid rock, it was necessary to remove all loose material until solid rock was reached. Work on the foundation excavations was completed in June 1933. During excavations for the foundations, approximately 1,500,000 yd^3 (1,150,000 m$^{3)}$ of material was removed, including material removed in canyon wall stripping operations.

To divert the river's flow around the construction site, four diversion tunnels were driven through the canyon walls, two on the Nevada side and two on the Arizona side. These tunnels were 56 feet (17.07 m) in diametre. Their combined length was nearly 16,000 feet (4877 m, more than three miles). Tunneling began at the lower portals of the Nevada tunnels in May 1931. Shortly after, work began on two similar tunnels in the Arizona canyon wall. In March 1932, work began on lining the tunnels with concrete. First the base or invert was poured. Gantry cranes, running on rails through the entire length of each tunnel were used to place the concrete. The sidewalls were poured next. Movable sections of steel forms were used for the sidewalls. Finally, using pneumatic guns, the overheads were filled in. The concrete lining is 3 feet (914.4 mm) thick, reducing the finished tunnel diametre to 50 ft (15.24 in).

Mount Rushmore National Memorial

Mount Rushmore National Memorial, near Keystone, South Dakota, is a monumental granite sculpture by Gutzon Borglum, located within the United States Presidential Memorial that represents the first 150 years of the history of the United States of America with 60-foot (18 m) sculptures of the heads of former United States presidents (left to right): George Washington (1732-1799), Thomas Jefferson (1743-1826), Theodore Roosevelt (1858-1919), and Abraham Lincoln (1809-1865). The entire memorial covers 1,278.45 acres (5.17 km^2) and is 5,725 feet (1,745 m) above sea level.

Mount Rushmore National Memorial

Between October 4, 1927, and October 31, 1941, Gutzon Borglum and 400 workers sculpted the colossal 60-foot (18 m) carvings of U.S. presidents George Washington, Thomas Jefferson,

Theodore Roosevelt, and Abraham Lincoln to represent the first 150 years of American history. These presidents were selected by Borglum because of their role in preserving the Republic and expanding its territory. The image of Thomas Jefferson was originally intended to appear in the area at Washington's right, but after the work there was begun, the rock was found unsuitable, so the work to that point on the Jefferson figure was dynamited, and a new figure was sculpted to Washington's left.

Ten years of redevelopment work culminated with the completion of extensive visitor facilities and sidewalks in 1998, such as a Visitor Centre, Museum, and the Presidential Trail. Maintenance of the memorial annually requires mountain climbers to monitor and seal cracks.

Mount Rushmore is largely composed of granite. The memorial is carved on the northwest margin of the Harney Peak granite batholith in the Black Hills of South Dakota, so the geologic formations of the heart of the Black Hills region are also evident at Mount Rushmore.

Borglum selected Mount Rushmore as the site for several reasons. The rock of the mountain is composed of smooth, fine-grained granite. The durable granite erodes only 1 inch (25 mm) every 10,000 years, indicating that it was sturdy enough to support sculpting. In addition, it was the tallest mountain in the region, looming to a height of 5,725 feet (1,745 m) above sea level. Because the mountain faces the southeast, the workers also had the advantage of sunlight for most of the day.

The Petronas Towers

The Petronas Twin Towers (also known as the Petronas Towers or Twin Towers), in Kuala Lumpur, Malaysia were the world's tallest buildings, before being surpassed by the Taipei 101. However, the towers are still the tallest twin buildings in the world.

The Petronas Towers

Designed by Argentine-American architect Cesar Pelli, the Petronas Towers were completed in 1998 and became the tallest buildings in the world on the date of completion. The

88-floor towers are constructed largely of reinforced concrete, with a steel and glass facade designed to resemble motifs found in Islamic art, a reflection of Malaysia's Muslim religion. They were built on the site of Kuala Lumpur's race track. Because of the depth of the bedrock, the buildings were built on the world's deepest foundations. The 120-metre foundations were built by Bachy Soletanche, and required massive amounts of concrete. In an unusual move, a different construction company was hired for each of the towers.

Due to a lack of steel and the huge cost of importing steel, the towers were constructed on a cheaper radical design of super high-strength reinforced concrete. High-strength concrete is a material familiar to Asian contractors and twice as effective as steel in sway reduction; however, it makes the building twice as heavy on its foundation than a comparable steel building. Supported by 23-by-23 metre concrete cores and an outer ring of widely-spaced super columns, the towers use a sophisticated structural system that accommodates its slender profile and provides from 1300 to 2000 square metres of column-free office space per floor. Spanning 17 acres below the building has the KLCC park with jogging and walking paths, a fountain with incorporated light show, wading pools, and a children's playground.

The towers feature a skybridge (constructed by Kukdong Engineering & Construction) between the two towers on 41st and 42nd floors, which is the highest 2-storey bridge in the world. The bridge is 170 m above the ground and 58 m long, weighing 750 tons. The same floor is also known as the podium, since visitors desiring to go to higher levels have to change elevators here. The skybridge also acts as a safety device, so that in the event of a fire or other emergency in one tower, tenants can evacuate by crossing the skybridge to the other tower.

Seven Forgotten Wonders of the Medieval Mind

Out of sight is out of mind – perhaps this has been the fate of the **Seven forgotten medieval wonders of the world**, which in the past had indeed inspired awe, admiration and respect in the heart of onlookers down the centuries after its creation but lost their importance to test of time. While some of these Seven forgotten medieval wonders of the world got eroded and destroyed to be converted to the state of ruins, some others lost in the competition with the more excellent works of human creativity and engineering feats that followed.

Medieval era around the world sparked the flame of intelligence and zeal for creativity, evident in the wondrous works of the time. But the turn of events and science since the time of the medieval to the modern world has been dramatic, leading to more extraordinary works, dwarfing the **marvels of the medieval world**.

Abu Simbel Temple

Abu Simbel is an archaeological site comprising two massive rock temples in southern Egypt on the western bank of Lake Nasser about 290 km southwest of Aswan. It is part of the UNESCO World Heritage Site known as the "Nubian Monuments", which run from Abu Simbel downriver to Philae.

Abu Simbel Temple

The twin temples were originally carved out of the mountainside during the reign of Pharaoh Ramesses II in the 13th century BC, as a lasting monument to himself and his queen Nefertari, to commemorate his alleged victory at the Battle of Kadesh, and to intimidate his Nubian neighbours. However, the complex was relocated in its entirety in the 1960s, on on an artificial hill made from a domed structure, high above the Aswan dam reservoir.

Construction of the temple complex started in approximately

1244 BC and lasted for about 20 years, until 1224 BC. Known as the "Temple of Ramses, beloved by Amun", it was one of six rock temples erected in Nubia during the long reign of Ramses II.

The Great Temple at Abu Simbel, which took about twenty wars to build, was completed around year 24 of the reign of Ramesses the Great. It was dedicated to the gods Amun Ra, Ra-Horakhty, and Ptah, as well as to the deified Ramesses himself. It is generally considered the grandest and most beautiful of the temples commissioned during the reign of Ramesses II, and one of the most beautiful in Egypt.

Four colossal 20 metre statues of the pharaoh with the double crown of Upper and Lower Egypt decorate the facade of the temple which is 35 metres wide and is topped by a frieze with 22 baboons, worshippers of the sun and flank the entrance. The colossal statues were sculptured directly from the rock in which the temple was located before it was moved.

The inner part of the temple has the same triangular layout that most ancient Egyptian temples follow, with rooms decreasing in size from the entrance to the sanctuary. The temple is complex in structure and quite unusual because of its many side chambers. The hypostyle hall (sometimes also called pronaos) is 18 metres long and 16.7 metres wide and is supported by eight huge Osirid pillars depicting the deified Ramesses linked to the god Osiris, the god of the Underworld, to indicate the everlasting nature of the pharaoh.

Angkor Wat

Angkor Wat (or Angkor Vat), is a temple at Angkor, Cambodia, built for King Suryavarman II in the early 12th century as his state temple and capital city. As the best-preserved temple at the site, it is the only one to have remained a significant religious centre since its foundation - first Hindu, dedicated to Vishnu, then Buddhist. The temple is the epitome of the high classical style of Khmer architecture. It has become a symbol of Cambodia, appearing on its national flag, and it is the country's prime attraction for visitors.

Angkor Wat

The outer wall, 1024 by 802 m and 4.5 m high, is surrounded by a 30 m apron of open ground and a moat 190 m wide. Access to the temple is by an earth bank to the east and a sandstone causeway to the west; the latter, the main entrance, is a later addition, possibly replacing a wooden bridge.

The outer wall encloses a space of 820,000 square metres (203 acres), which besides the temple proper was originally occupied by the city and, to the north of the temple, the royal palace. Like all secular buildings of Angkor, these were built of perishable materials rather than of stone, so nothing remains of them except the outlines of some of the streets. A 350 m causeway connects the western gopura to the temple proper, with naga balustrades and six sets of steps leading down to the city on either side.

The temple stands on a terrace raised higher than the city. It is made of three rectangular galleries rising to a central tower, each level higher than the last. Mannikka interprets these galleries as being dedicated to the king, Brahma, the moon, and Vishnu. Each gallery has a gopura at each of the points, and the two inner galleries each have towers at their corners, forming a quincunx with the central tower. Because the temple faces west, the features are all set back towards the east, leaving more space to be filled in each enclosure and gallery on the west side; for the same reason the west-facing steps are shallower than those on the other sides.

The outer gallery measures 187 by 215 m, with pavilions rather than towers at the corners. The gallery is open to the outside of the temple, with columned half-galleries extending and buttressing the structure.

Taj Mahal of Agra

The Taj Mahal, is a mausoleum located in Agra, India, that was built under Mughal Emperor Shah Jahan in memory of his favourite wife, Mumtaz Mahal. While the white domed marble and tile mausoleum is most familiar, Taj Mahal is an integrated symmetric complex of structures that was completed around 1648. Ustad Ahmad Lahauri is generally considered to be the principal designer of the Taj Mahal.

Taj Mahal of Agra

The focus of the Taj Mahal is the white marble tomb, which stands on a square plinth consisting of a symmetrical building with an iwan, an arch-shaped doorway, topped by a large dome. Like most Mughal tombs, basic elements are Persian in origin.

The base of the Taj is a large, multi-chambered structure.

The base structure is a large, multi-chambered structure. The base is essentially a cube with chamfered edges and is roughly 55 metres on each side. On the long sides, a massive pishtaq, or vaulted archway, frames the diwan with a similar arch-shaped balcony.

The interior chamber of the Taj Mahal steps far beyond traditional decorative elements. Here the inlay work is not pietra dura, but lapidary of precious and semiprecious gemstones. The inner chamber is an octagon with the design allowing for entry from each face, though only the south garden-facing door is used. The interior walls are about 25 metres high and topped by a "false" interior dome decorated with a sun motif. Eight pishtaq arches define the space at ground level. As with the exterior, each lower pishtaq is crowned by a second pishtaq about midway up the wall.

The four central upper arches form balconies or viewing areas and each balcony's exterior window has an intricate screen or jali cut from marble. In addition to the light from the balcony screens, light enters through roof openings covered by chattris at the corners. Each chamber wall has been highly decorated with dado bas relief, intricate lapidary inlay and refined calligraphy panels, reflecting in miniature detail the design elements seen throughout the exterior of the complex. The octagonal marble screen or jali which borders the cenotaphs is made from eight marble panels. Each panel has been carved through with intricate pierce work. The remaining surfaces have been inlaid with semiprecious stones in extremely delicate detail, forming twining vines, fruits and flowers.

Mont Saint-Michel

Mont Saint-Michel is a rocky tidal island in Normandy, France. It is located approximately one kilometre off the country's north coast, at the mouth of the Couesnon River near Avranches.

Mont Saint-Michel was used in the sixth and seventh centuries as an Armorican stronghold of Romano-Breton culture and power, until it was ransacked by the Franks, thus ending the trans-channel culture that had stood since the departure of the Romans in AD 460.

Mont Saint-Michel

Mont Saint-Michel was previously connected to the mainland via a thin natural land bridge, which before modernization was covered at high tide and revealed at low tide. Thus, Mont Saint-Michel has been compromised by several developments.

Over the centuries, the coastal flats have been polderised to create pasture. Thus the distance between the shore and the south coast of Mont- Saint-Michel has decreased.

Before the construction of the first monastic establishment in the 8th century, the island was called Mont Tombe.

According to legend, the archangel Michael appeared to St. Aubert, bishop of Avranches, in 708 and instructed him to build a church on the rocky islet. Aubert repeatedly ignored the angel's instruction, until Michael burned a hole in the bishop's skull with his finger.

The mount gained strategic significance in 933 when William "Long Sword", Duke of Normandy, annexed the Cotentin Peninsula, definitively placing the mount in Normandy. It is depicted in the Bayeux Tapestry, which commemorates the 1066 Norman conquest of England. Ducal patronage financed the spectacular Norman architecture of the abbey in subsequent centuries.

In 1067, the monastery of Mont Saint-Michel gave its support to duke William of Normandy in his claim to the throne of England. It was rewarded with properties and grounds on the English side of the Channel, including a small island located at the west of Cornwall, which, modelled after the Mount, became a Norman priory named St Michael's Mount of Penzance.

During the Hundred Years' War the, English made repeated assaults on the island but were unable to seize it, partly due to the abbey's improved fortifications. Les Michelettes, two wrought-iron bombards left by the English in their failed 1423-24 siege of Mont Saint-Michel, are still displayed near the outer defense wall.

The Moai Statues

Moai are monolithic human figures carved from rock on the Polynesian island of Rapa Nui (Easter Island) between 1250 and 1500 CE. Nearly half are still at Rano Raraku, the main Moai quarry, but hundreds were transported from there and set on stone platforms called Ahu around the island's perimetre. Almost all Moai have overly large heads three-fifths the size of their bodies. The Moai are chiefly the 'living faces' (aringa ora) of deified ancestors. The statues still gazed inland across their clan lands when Europeans first visited the island, but most would be cast down during later conflicts between clans.

The Moai Statues

The statues' production and transportation is considered a remarkable intellectual, creative, and physical feat. The tallest Moai erected, called Paro, was almost 10 metres (33 ft) high and weighed 75 tonnes; the heaviest erected was a shorter but squatter Moai at Ahu Tonganki, weighing 86 tons; and one unfinished sculpture, if completed, would have been approximately 21 metres (69 ft) tall with a weight of about 270 tons.

The Moai are monolithic statues, their minimalist style related to forms found throughout Polynesia. Moai are carved in relatively flat planes, the faces bearing proud but enigmatic expressions. The over-large heads have heavy brows, elongated noses with a distinctive fish-hook shaped curl of the nostrils.

The lips protrude in a thin pout. Like the nose, the ears are elongated, and oblong in form. The jaw lines stand out against the truncated neck. The torsos are heavy, and sometimes the clavicles are subtly outlined in stone. The arms are carved in bas relief and rest against the body in various positions, hands and long slender fingers resting along the crests of the hips, meeting at the hami (loincloth), with the thumbs sometimes pointing towards the navel. Generally, the anatomical details of the backs are not detailed, but sometimes bear a ring and girdle motif on the buttocks and lower back. Except for one kneeling Moai, the statues do not have legs.

All but 53 of the 887 Moai known to date were carved from tuff (a compressed volcanic ash). At the end of carving they would rub the statue with pumice from Rano Raraku, where 394 Moai and incomplete Moai are still visible today (there are also 13 Moai carved from basalt, 22 from trachyte and 17 from fragile red scoria).

The Parthenon of Athens

The Acropolis of Athens is the best known acropolis (high city, The "Sacred Rock") in the world. Although there are many other acropoleis in Greece, the significance of the Acropolis of Athens is such that it is commonly known as The Acropolis without qualification. The Acropolis was formally proclaimed is the pre-eminent monument on the European Cultural Heritage list of monuments on 26 March 2007. The Acropolis is a flat-topped rock which rises 150 m (490 ft) above sea level in the city of Athens. It was also known as Cecropia, after the legendary serpent-man, Kekrops or Cecrops, the first Athenian king.

The Parthenon of Athens

Once into the Bronze Age, there is little doubt that a Mycenaean megaron must have stood on top of the hill, housing the local potentate and his household, guards, the local cult facilities and a number of workshops and ordinary habitations.

The compound was surrounded by a thick Cyclopean circuit wall, possibly between 4.5 m and 6 m in height, consisting of two parapets built with large stone blocks and cemented with an earth mortar called emplekton. The wall follows typical Mycenaean convention in that its gate was arranged obliquely, with a parapet and tower overhanging the incomers' right-hand side, thus facilitating defense. There were two lesser approaches up the hill on its north side, consisting of steep, narrow flights of steps cut in the rock.

Most of the major temples were rebuilt under the leadership of Pericles during the Golden Age of Athens (460-430 BC). Phidias, a great Athenian sculptor, and Ictinus and Callicrates, two famous architects, were responsible for the reconstruction. During the 5th century BC, the Acropolis gained its final shape.

The entrance to the Acropolis was a monumental gateway called the Propylaea. To the south of the entrance is the tiny Temple of Athena Nike. A bronze statue of Athena, sculpted by Phidias, originally stood at its centre. At the centre of the Acropolis is the Parthenon or Temple of Athena Parthenon (Athena the Virgin). East of the entrance and north of the Parthenon is the temple known as the Erechtheum. South of the platform that forms the top of the Acropolis there are also the remains of an outdoor theatre called Theatre of Dionysus. A few hundred metres away, there is the now partially reconstructed Theatre of Herodes Atticus.

The Shwedagon Pagoda

The Shwedagon Pagoda, also known as the Golden Pagoda, is a 98-metre (approx. 321.5 feet) gilded stupa located in Yangon, Burma. The pagoda lies to the west of Kandawgyi Lake, on Singuttara Hill, thus dominating the skyline of the city. It is the most sacred Buddhist pagoda for the Burmese with relics of the past four Buddhas enshrined within, namely the staff of

The Shwedagon Pagoda

Kakusandha, the water filter of Konagamana, a piece of the robe of Kassapa and eight hairs of Gautama, the historical Buddha.

Legend has it that the Shwedagon Pagoda is 2500 years old. Archaeologists believe the stupa was actually built sometime between the 6th and 10th centuries by the Mon, but this is a very controversial issue because according to the records by Buddhist monks it was built before Lord Buddha died in 486 BC.

There are four entrances (mouk) to the Paya that lead up a flight of steps to the platform (yin byin) on Siriguttara Hill. The eastern and southern approaches have vendors selling books, good luck charms, Buddha images, candles, gold leaf, incense sticks, prayer flags, streamers, miniature umbrellas and flowers. A pair of giant chinthe (leogryphs, mythical lions) guard the entrances and the image in the shrine at the top of the steps from the south is that of the second Buddha, Konagamana. The base or plinth of the stupa is made of bricks covered with gold plates. Above the base are terraces (pyissayan) that only monks and men can access. Next is the bell-shaped part (khaung laung bon) of the stupa. Above that is the turban (baung yit), then the inverted almsbowl (thabeik), inverted and upright lotus petals (kya hmauk kya hlan), the banana bud (nga pyaw bu) and then the crown. The crown or umbrella (hti) is tipped with 5,448 diamonds and 2,317 rubies. The very top, the diamond bud (sein bu) is tipped with a 76 carat (15 g) diamond.

The Gold seen on the stupa is made of genuine gold plates, covering the brick structure attached by traditional rivets. Myanmar people all over the country, as well as monarchs in its history, have donated gold to the pagoda to maintain it. It was started in the 15th century by the Mon Queen Shin Sawbu who gave her weight in gold and continues to this day.

www.ingramcontent.com/pod-product-compliance
Lightning Source LLC
Chambersburg PA
CBHW070336230426
43663CB00011B/2336